THE DISCOVERY OF *joy*

Also by Richard Eyre

Spiritual Serendipity
Stewardship of the Heart
Lifebalance (with Linda J. Eyre)
Teaching Your Children Values (with Linda J. Eyre)
The Awakening (a novel)
What Manner of Man
How to Talk to Your Child about Sex (with Linda J. Eyre)
Teaching Your Children Joy (with Linda J. Eyre)
3 Steps to a Strong Family (with Linda J. Eyre)
Don't Just Do Something, Sit There
The Wrappings and the Gifts
Teaching Your Children Responsibility (with Linda J. Eyre)
The Birth That We Call Death (with Paul H. Dunn)
The Secret of the Sabbath
Teaching Your Children Sensitivity (with Linda J. Eyre)
Children's Stories to Teach Joy (with Linda J. Eyre)
Alexander's Amazing Adventures: Values for Children (audiotape
series, with Linda J. Eyre)
Relationships: Self, God, Family (with Paul H. Dunn)
Simplified Husbandship/Simplified Fathership
Free to Be Free
The Change That We Call Birth
Lifeplanning (with Paul H. Dunn)
I Challenge You/I Promise You (with Paul H. Dunn)
Utah in the Year 2000
Goals (with Paul H. Dunn)

NEW YORK TIMES #1 BESTSELLING AUTHOR

RICHARD EYRE

THE DISCOVERY OF *joy*

REVISED EDITION

BOOKCRAFT

SALT LAKE CITY, UTAH

Library of Congress Catalog Card Number: 00-130362

Printed in the United States of America   54459-6665

10   9   8   7   6   5   4   3   2   1

Contents

Foreword vii

Preface ix

1. The Most Important Word 1

2. A Model for Joy 5
   Its Levels, Components, and Sources

3. The Vehicle of Joy 21
   Second Estate: Earth, Bodies, Agency

4. The Pursuit of Joy 1 46

5. The Enhancers or Prompters of Joy 58
   Relationships and Achievements

6. The Pursuit of Joy 2 76

7. The Expander of Joy 109
   Knowledge and Truth

8. The Pursuit of Joy 3 127

9. The Sealer of Joy 141
   Righteousness and the Holy Ghost

10. The Pursuit of Joy 4 158

Postscript: Try It! 171

Foreword

When I first met Richard, his favorite word was *joy*. And it still is.

The reason I wanted first to date him and later to marry him is that I felt more joy with him than with anyone else. When our first children were born, we decided our goal for their early years—more important than preschool academics—was to enhance the joy they came with. That goal led to our first co-authored book, *Teaching Your Children Joy,* and to *Joy Schools*—do-it-yourself, at-home preschools that have now involved more than 100,000 parents and children.* Richard has made *joy* the byword of our marriage, of our parenting, and of our careers. Joy, in its full definition, is the objective of this life, and it has long been Richard's criterion for what he does or doesn't do.

So you might say we've had a long history of joy. In this book, Richard has, I believe, made the word and its deeper meanings more accessible. To him, joy encompasses and supersedes happiness and sorrow. It is both something we can receive and something we can earn, both something that is all around us for the taking and something we gain only after struggle and sacrifice. In all cases, though, it is born of awareness and of faith, and it is always a matter of the heart and of the spirit.

Linda J. Eyre

*For information about Joy Schools, call (801) 581-0112, or visit valuesparenting.com on the Internet.

Preface

Joy, often incompletely perceived as happiness,
is too often thought of as a *mood*
that comes by chance or circumstance.
Herein we will deal with it as a *mode*
that can be adopted
and as a gift that can be pursued.

Happiness, or some synonym, is sought by all people. Some seek it
consciously; all seek it subconsciously.

Volumes have been written on what it is, and on where and how to
find it.

Every religion and every philosophy talks of it, focuses on it, tries
to show the way to get it.

Every thinking man or woman has some views on it, and wants to
have more of it.

*One might therefore say, "Well, if so much has been thought, so much
written on happiness . . . then why another volume?"*

*First, because there is something higher and stronger and more eternal
than happiness . . . which we will call joy.*

*Second, because only in the fullness of the gospel of Jesus Christ
(which has been not long restored) can we find a full definition of joy
(and a full explanation of where and how it can be found).*

Gospel means good news. In fact, *gospel* means glad tidings
of great joy.
Therefore one who believes that the fullness of the gospel has been
restored

should also believe that the fullness of joy has been restored.
I believe it has; I believe that the gospel of Jesus Christ is a perfect
blueprint for joy.
I believe that mortality, this earth, and our physical bodies
were gifts from our Heavenly Father.

This book makes no attempt to create a new philosophy or even to
propose new answers.
Rather, it attempts to collect and organize and clarify
the insights and truths regarding joy
that have already been revealed from God.

I've been thinking and writing about joy
for most of my life.
In fact, a precursor, an earlier edition,
was published way back in 1974.
When I wrote it, still in my twenties,
I felt a certain awe and wonder
which I've tried to preserve
(in my life and in this book).

The broken line, poetry/prose style
has two intents:
1. To let thoughts flow and sometimes
stay open-ended, rather than confining
them to conclusions and paragraphs.
2. To leave some white space on every page
where you can do your own writing.
Read with a pen,
make your own notes and observations,
become a co-author with me
as we explore joy together.

If there was ever a time for re-reassessment,
for review, revision, and personal renewal,
it is the start of a new millennium.
May we all, each in our own way,
but sharing our thoughts as we go,
seek and find more love
and more joy.

Richard Eyre
Spring 2000
Bear Lake, Idaho

1

The Most Important Word

Let me tell you some experiences I had
during one week:

On Sunday three separate speakers in church,
in three separate talks, quoted:
"Men are, that they might have joy" (2 Nephi 2:25),
and they each used it in a slightly different context.

On my Monday way to work, the radio played Bach's
"Jesu, Joy of Man's Desiring,"
and the announcer shortened the title to
"Joy."

On Tuesday, I read my patriarchal blessing and noticed
(as I often had before)
that one of the three admonitions it contains is to
"develop joy and gladness."

At lunch on Wednesday, an associate told me that
Joseph Smith had said that joy
was the main objective of our lives.[1]

Thursday night I went to a reference book to
document my friend's statement . . .
found that it was essentially true,
and also found that Brigham Young had said
"We are [here] to learn how to enjoy";[2]
and that Parley P. Pratt had said
"Intelligence exists in order to enjoy."[3]

---

1. "Happiness is the object and design of our existence." *Teachings of the Prophet Joseph Smith,* sel. Joseph Fielding Smith (Deseret Book, 1938), p. 255.
2. *Discourses of Brigham Young,* comp. John A. Widtsoe (Deseret Book, 1971), p. 237.
3. *Key to Theology* (Deseret Book, 1955), p. 63.

Friday I had lunch at a restaurant
called the "Sans Souci"
and was told that the name was French for
"Joy . . . without care or worry."

I sat down that Sunday
and wondered
why the word
Joy
had been bumping its way into my mind all week.

I decided
to make a serious study of the word . . .
to try to find out exactly what it means,

       exactly what its components are,
       exactly what its sources are,
       exactly where and how
       it can be sought
       and found.

The study lasted more than a year
and led me to ten conclusions about joy:

1.   That it is the most important word in all languages;
      that it is a far deeper and broader and more important
      word than *happiness.*

          2.   That it is a one-word summary
                  of the purpose of life; and that it is not
                  possible without mortality.

     3.   That "joy" is the positive and correct
           interpretation and application
           of this life's experience . . . all of it.

4.   That the amount of joy one
has is in direct proportion to the
righteousness of his
life.

5.   That joy includes
(and in fact is impossible without)
suffering and temptation and adversity . . .
that joy and sorrow
are as much related as
joy and pleasure.

6.   That joy is something that *can be*
aspired to and sought after
and obtained.

7.   That an additional interpretation of 2 Nephi 2:25
might be:
"Adam fell that men might become *mortal,*
and men
are mortal that they might have *experience*" . . .
(all experience, within the gospel's light,
can be linked to joy).

8.   That God designed this earth with the objective
of providing the ultimate environment or climate for joy.

9.   That joy has some discernible
components that can be individually
obtained and then combined.

10. That seeking joy is the most important
and the most eternally rewarding activity
in life (and is synonymous with
"working out our own salvation").

When you finish this book,
turn back to these ten conclusions
and see if you agree with each of them.

2

A Model for Joy

Its Levels, Components, and Sources

What Is Joy?

Some questions have answers on several different levels.
To ask, "What is joy?" is a little like asking,
"What is a house?"

Four walls and a roof are a house,
but when electricity and plumbing and heating are added
it is more of a house;
when furniture and fixtures are added
it is still more of a house;
> and when a loving family is added, it is so much
> more of a house
> that it becomes a home.

Similarly, joy exists on four levels.

Imagine first a man, standing alone in a valley,
his head turned east to watch a sunrise.
As the top of the sun's dome appears,
he feels its warm rays chase the night's coldness
from the stiff muscles of his body.
> His eyes see the clouds turning gold.
> His ears hear the meadowlark welcome the sun.
> His nose breathes the freshness and tastes the sage,
> > and his heart quickens as he anticipates
> > the freedom of a new day.

He feels joy . . .
It is a physical joy, a temporal pleasure,
        and the *vehicle* of the joy is *the earth,*
                            and his body,
                            and his agency . . .
and the joy is real, but it is not full.

Let's call it "Joy 1."

Now change the scene slightly
(or should we say greatly)
by putting his wife next to him,
        a wife soon to have a child,
                    her hand in his . . .
and by putting a home behind them,
        a log cabin, let's say,
                built by his own hands.

He knows that the wife whose hand he holds
                    feels what he feels.
He loves her,
he protects her and he protects the baby . . .
and the house behind him he has built for them.

He feels greater joy because there is an emotional and
social element
added to the physical . . .
and these *enhancers* of his joy
are his *relationships*
and his *achievements.*

Let's call it "Joy 2."

Now shift again.
Let the man accept the truth and understanding
        of the fullness of the gospel . . .
the faith and knowledge that tell him that,

because of the love and atonement of Jesus Christ,
they can be exalted and live together eternally
        (his wife, his child, and he).

Give him the truth that testifies that the baby in
his wife's womb came from a preexistence
where they (the parents) also originated . . .
        and let him understand the purpose of his life and know
        that the world on which he stands
        and the sun that he watches were made
                                by a loving God
                                for him,
                                and for the second estate
                                of him and his family.

He now feels still greater joy
because the mental/spiritual aspect of comprehending truth
has been added to the physical, emotional, and social . . .
and the *expander*
of his joy is the *insight*
                and *knowledge* that the gospel gives.

        This third level of joy . . .
        joy that includes the *vehicle*, the *enhancers*,
        and the *expander* . . .
        is "Joy 3."

Now,
one final addition to the scene.

Add the Holy Ghost's presence.
Make the man a righteous and prayerful man
        who obeys the Lord and who has received
        the Holy Ghost through the priesthood
        and by the laying on of hands.

This Spirit calms him, comforts him, strengthens him,
and gives him truth.
It turns all that he feels and all that he knows
from shallow and temporary to deep and eternal.

Through the Holy Ghost he knows that his life
harmonizes with his purpose.

He begins to feel Christ's acceptance and pleasure in his effort,
the sure, strong starting of sanctification,
and his feelings take on a spiritual quality that
purifies
and magnifies the joy he feels.

The *sealer* of the joy is
        the Spirit of the Lord,

and we call this highest level
"Joy 4."

Four elements of joy . . .
Four levels of the word . . .

and each of us has access to all.

But to say that each has access to joy
is not to say that all *have* joy,
for there is an *effort* aspect to each level of joy.

Although Joy 1 and Joy 3 are essentially *gifts,*
we must actively *receive, accept,* and *appreciate.*
And Joy 2 and Joy 4 must be
developed, preserved, created.

To feel Joy 1 we must *tune* our appreciation
and our senses
and our awareness,
thus maintaining and improving our *vehicle* of joy.

To feel Joy 2 we must *develop* loving relationships
and *pursue* relevant accomplishment,
thus finding and engaging the *enhancers* or *prompters*.

To feel Joy 3 we must *learn* and *discover* and *seek* truth
through mental and spiritual channels.
We must receive and accept by faith,
thus acquiring the insight, the knowledge
that is the extender and the *expander* of joy.

Finally, to feel Joy 4 we must become obedient enough
and righteous enough
to have the Spirit accompany us and tell us
that our lives are acceptable to God.
We must work out our own salvation, seeking sanctification, and
thus
merit the presence of the *sealer* of joy.

The circular, clockwise diagram on the next page
illustrates the sequence and the connections of the four levels of joy,
and shows the ties
        between the vehicle
        and the enhancers
        and the extender
        and the sealer.

A Model for Joy

1. The Vehicle of Joy
Our second estate—
earth, bodies, agency
(physical)

2. The Enhancers or Prompters
Relationships and
accomplishments
(social/emotional)

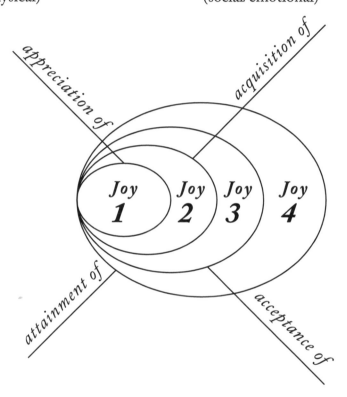

4. The Sealer of Joy
Righteousness and
the Holy Ghost
(Spiritual)

3. The Expander of Joy
Knowledge, truth,
and testimony
(mental/spiritual)

As you think about the model, note a couple of things:
1.   Each level of joy is encompassed by the next level.
        (Joy 2 uses and builds on Joy 1.)
2.   Levels 1 and 3 are about *appreciating* and *accepting*—
        about *receiving* (actively and fully)
        what God gives us.
While levels 2 and 4 are about *acquiring* and *obtaining*—
about using the gifts of levels 1 and 3
to create or bring to pass levels 2 and 4.

Once the four-element model is in mind,
it is relatively easy to categorize
all recognized sources
of joy
into one of the four levels.

Joy 1 is the physical and temporal pleasure and experience
of this earth.

Joy 1 includes:

The joy of work.

The joy of nature and animals . . . the earth's wonder
and beauty.

The joy of agency and choice and self-determination.

The joy of health and of physical gifts and talents.

The joy of physical pleasure or comfort.

Joy 1 is not less important than
or inferior to other kinds of joy.
In fact,
in one way of thinking, it is the most important,
        since it is a prerequisite for all the others.

As a *level* of joy, however, it *is* inferior,
because,
by itself,
it can never reach the pitch or the depth or the height
of Joy 2 or Joy 3 or Joy 4.

Joy 2
is Joy 1
with the enhancers or prompters
of relationships and accomplishments
added.

It includes:

The joy of family.

The joy of communication.

The joy of humor.

The joy of sharing and empathy.

The joy of service.

The joy of creating and building and goal-striving.

The joy of well-made decisions and correct choices.

The joy of being appreciated.

Joy 1, the vehicle of joy,
is to some degree a joy in and of itself . . .
  just as an automotive vehicle is somewhat of a joy
  just sitting in a driveway
        looking new.

But when the enhancer of joy is added to the vehicle,
joy is affected in the same way
as the automobile is affected when one gets in and drives.

Joy 3 is Joy 2 *expanded*
by the addition of *gospel insight and knowledge.*

Joy 3 adds the mental element and lends the truth
that makes joy understandable
and preservable.

It includes a deepening of all that is Joy 2 . . . and adds:

The joy of learning and of discovering new truth.

The joy of knowing which priorities are correct.

The joy of knowing purpose and understanding foreordination.

The joy of the true freedom that comes from truth.

The joy of insight into origin, purpose, and destiny.

If Joy 2
is like being in the car, driving it . . .
Joy 3
is like *knowing where* you are going,
and *why* you are going there,
and *how* the car operates in getting you there.

Joy 4 is Joy 3 sealed by the presence
of the Holy Ghost.

Joy 4
envelopes all other joy
as an atmosphere shrouds an earth,
and it turns earthly, temporary joy
into heavenly, eternal joy.

Joy 4 is built around:

The joy of faith and true, communicating prayer.

The joy of temple principles and covenants.

The joy of the use of the priesthood and of dependency on the Spirit.

The joy of sure testimony and spiritual knowledge.

The joy of light and of upper-level opening of mind.

The joy of working out your own salvation.

The joy of the Atonement and of its sanctification.

The joy of feeling God's pleasure and his assurance.

The joy of ultimate confidence in self as a son or daughter of Heavenly Father.

Joy 4 is like having a father who
approves
of how you drive the car,
who approves of your appreciation and understanding of the car,
and who tells you that it is yours
to keep.

Only Joy 4 is independent of circumstances and free
of the world.

Joy 1, Joy 2, and Joy 3 can exist
                only under favorable circumstances.

In moments of pleasure or beauty,
                Joy 1 can flourish,
but in moments of suffering or ugliness,
                Joy 1 can disappear.

In moments of success or love,
                Joy 2 can flourish,
but in moments of failure and loss,
                Joy 2 can disappear.

In moments of inspiration and enlightenment,
                Joy 3 can flourish,
but in moments of disillusion and doubt,
                Joy 3 can disappear.

But Joy 4 is true and full joy . . .
complete enough to be independent of circumstances.
In the presence of its four elements,
                all earthly experience is positive.

When one is hurt or sick or confined,
it is the perspective and comfort
of the Spirit
that gets him through—
learning all the way
            (as with Job).

When one fails or loses, it is
his knowledge of this earth's purpose
and the presence of the Comforter that
brings him the joy
of growth
and of understanding
        (as with Joseph Smith).

And when one is troubled or confused, it is
the Holy Ghost that molds
his gospel knowledge
into personal, workable testimony and solutions
of joy
        (as with Enos).

The most complete and meaningful use of the word *joy*
is in its use as Joy 4.

Joy 4:

is the object and design of our existence.[1]

is the purpose for which we exist.[2]

encompasses all of life's experience, including temptation
and affliction (James 1:2).

is a word that is, in fact, synonymous with
the kingdom of God (Romans 14:17).

cannot be taken away by any man (John 16:22).

Thus a man or woman who reaches the level of Joy 4
can find joy in all aspects of life.

---

1. *Teachings of the Prophet Joseph Smith*, p. 255.
2. Parley P. Pratt, *Key to Theology*, p. 63.

And from that level *all* of life's experiences
                    can include *all four* types
                    of joy
(for Joy 4 implies that we have developed the capacity
                    to receive each).

All experience,
from a birth to a funeral
and everything in between,
                    can then yield joy.

The Pursuit of Joy and the Goals of This Book

There are two widespread and unfortunate misconceptions
about joy.

The first and deepest one is that joy is a thing
of the hereafter,
unavailable on this earth,
that we must struggle through mortality to get to joy.

Yet God says joy is mortality's goal (2 Nephi 2:25).
Would he design an earth where our eternal purpose was
thwarted or undermined?
          No.

          Joy is present and possible on this earth.
          Not the fullness of resurrected, celestial joy (D&C 93:33),
          but a prerequisite joy that leads to fullness,
          a happiness great enough that
when we contemplated it in the preexistence
          it made us shout for joy (Job 38:7).

The second misconception is heard even more frequently.
It is the belief that joy cannot or should not be sought . . .
    that those who pursue it will never find it . . .
    that it comes only to those
        who are not consciously seeking it.

    Not so.
    It *can* be sought; it should be sought.
    It can be found; it should be found.

    When Joseph Smith called happiness
    "the object and design of our existence,"
    he promised that those who pursue it properly . . .
    who look in the right places . . .
    will find it.[3]

The reason for the
"you-can't-find-it-if-you-seek-it" misconception
is that so many have sought joy
and *failed* to find it.

But the reason for their failure is not that
joy cannot be successfully sought;
rather, it is that they have made one or both
of the following mistakes
in the *way* that they pursued joy.

1. Looking in the wrong places.
    So many look to worldly pleasures and possessions instead of
        to the appreciation and use of body,
        earth, and agency;
        the attainment of true relationships
        and relevant achievements;
        the acquisition of eternal truth and knowledge;
        the acceptance and presence of the Holy Ghost.

---

3. *Teachings of the Prophet Joseph Smith*, pp. 255–56.

2. Seeking the four levels of joy in the wrong order.
     Seeking Joy 2 before you have Joy 1
     is like plowing without a plow.
     The four levels of joy are *consecutive* and sequential:
          that is, number one *precedes*
               and is *prerequisite* to number two.

As the Joy model shows, the Joy 1 of
appreciation and use of bodies and earth and agency
motivates and combines with relationships and achievement
to form Joy 2,
which in turn can awaken a desire for understanding
and then join with it in the circle of Joy 3.
The light of Joy 3 can motivate righteousness and the reception
of the Holy Ghost, which can, with our devotion,
lift Joy 3 into the higher realm of Joy 4.

So joy *is* available on this earth,
and we *can* successfully seek it.

In light of these two facts,
this book has eight objectives:

1.   To describe and discuss the vehicle of joy,
        (earth, bodies, agency) clearly and compellingly
        so that you (the reader) will *want* Joy 1
        enough to pursue it.

           2.   To suggest effective methods
                   for the pursuit of Joy 1.

3.   To similarly discuss the enhancers or prompters of joy
        (relationships and achievements).

           4.   To suggest patterns for the pursuit of Joy 2.

5.   To similarly discuss the expander of joy
       (truth and knowledge).

         6.   To suggest approaches to the pursuit of Joy 3.

7.   To similarly discuss the sealer of joy
       (righteousness and the Holy Ghost).

         8.   To suggest commitments to the pursuit of
                Joy 4.

Each of the eight goals
makes up
one of the remaining eight chapters.

3

The Vehicle of Joy
Second Estate: Earth, Bodies, Agency

The Vehicle of Joy

Our second estate—
earth, bodies, agency
(physical)

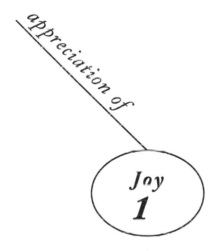

Six Stories: Part One

"The Flower and the Camera"—Part One

Imagine a single, simple, startlingly beautiful flower.
See the delicate perfection of its petals;
smell its sweet scent;
gently touch its green stem;
revel in the joy of its beauty

and your capacity to experience it,
a tiny, vivid taste of Joy 1.
(to be continued)

"The First Lawn Mowing"—Part One

Two little boys,
mowing their lawn for the first time.
It takes both to push the mower,
one on each side of the handle.
The thick spring grass resists its first cutting of the year,
but the boys persist,
and the stretch of arms and legs
and the beauty that nature provided and they enhanced
gives them Joy 1.
(to be continued)

"The Love Story"—Part One

John and Mary met in a biology class in the spring.
On their first date the world became Camelot.
They sat under a blossom-laden apple tree
and held hands while the sun set.
The touch of their fingers seemed to have its own
source of energy.
There was a magnetic field pulling them together,
blurring their vision, making their hearts pound.
Some days later, when they kissed for the first time,
they saw stars and heard bells.
Each other's physical presence made care and worry disappear,
and physical contact brought an ecstasy
that neither could explain.
It was Joy 1.
(to be continued)

"The Marriage"—Part One

Kneeling across an altar of marriage
in a temple of God.
Sun streaming diagonally
from a high corner window behind him,
intersecting the crystal of the chandelier,
passing over their heads and splashing the thick rug behind her.
Outside its beam . . . soft light in soft silence.
Her purity enhanced by white lace but
focused in the clear light of her eyes across from
his square-jawed strength.
Two bodies filled with health and vibrance,
touching now only at the hand, but that touch
like an electrical connection,
lighting both faces and tingling each toe.
The anticipation of physical intimacy reserved and protected
to follow this moment, this ceremony
and the excitement of agency
to walk forth from this place and choose their own life.
(to be continued)

"The New Arrival"—Part One

Nine months of physical changes . . .
some senses expanded, others depressed . . .
feeling the miracle of new human life inside.
Finally labor . . . the unique experience of exquisite pain . . .
so intense that you couldn't bear it if
it were for any other reason.
Then hearing the first cry,
counting the fingers and toes,
marveling at the tiny perfect human that your bodies
have helped to make.
Lying in the hospital room the next day
holding her, just fed, contented . . .
sunlight sifting in from the golden autumn day . . .
anticipating the freedom of raising her your way.
(to be continued)

The hair stood up on his neck,
a wave of pure pleasure
as he entered the chairman's office.
He'd been summoned, and the news had to be good.
The chairman smile, handed him an envelope,
and said, "Congratulations."
Even before opening it, there was joy
in the feel of the creamy, quality paper of the envelope,
the rich rosewood desk top,
the warm tingle in his spine.
The first joy was physical celebration.
(to be continued)

Physical joy . . .
our *bodies,* our *earth,* and our *agency* . . . the vehicle
for joy . . . the essence of Joy 1.
Let's look at each of these three parts of the vehicle.

Earth

Ponder for a moment
the joys of this world . . .
The joys that, in their premortal contemplation,
caused us to shout for joy.

Think about some of the things
        that make this world a place of wonder and joy.
Let your mind open . . . envision a few small parts of the earth
        as they are described.

Think first of the joy of the rare and beautiful days that
come with the changing of the season . . .

They come only a few times
each year,
in spring and in autumn . . .
the change days,
the vivid days,
the clear, crisp, alive days,
the "seldom days."
You can feel them . . .
sky's blue, tree's green
(or fire orange) . . .
more contrast . . .
eyes see further, better . . .
alive senses . . . the air makes you tingle and
it's early morning all day.
Things wrong in life seem little
because
good things are so big and so all around and real.

Next, think of a sunset . . .
clouds,
cool, white-blue at their highest,
in the middle of the
sky,
then with orange bottoms further
toward the west. . . .
Brighter, redder, finally
glowing
as the clouds
meet the mountains
which contain the sun.

Now think of the joy of animals,
of our attraction to the other creatures
with whom we share this earth.
A joy hard to explain because it traces back to a preexistence
that we can't remember . . .

a place where they
were made spiritually.
An affinity hard to explain but easy to see
in a little boy next door with a new pet,
a duck that he follows and feeds
and falls asleep with in his hammock.
When I saw him there the other day,

I could see his joy
right through his sleep.

Now let spring come into your mind,
and look out of the dripping green rectangle
of your window . . .

Watch the sky-open rain
                    in mid-April
as the Lord oversees the perennial process
of replacing death with life.

Sunny days are bright, careless and secure . . .
        but the
        moody, stirring bluster of
        slinging branches, sliding clouds,
        lash-splatter raindrops,
        has more depth, more
        meaning,
        and awakens the minor scales,
                    the diminished chords
        of your mind.

Then the light of the evening sky
turns soft,
and somehow warm,
even through the streaming water beads . . .
and gradually the violence of the thunderstorm
                                is subdued
by the soft glow of the sky

and it recedes to gentle pattering
more in tune with the mood dictated
                              by the sky. . . .
The clouds roll back and in a few moments
the sky responds
by producing a blue as delicate and pale
as the roof
of heaven.

Think of the experiences and moods of our world . . .
Come now into a high mountain forest.
The coat of the horse under you glistens . . .
There's a mood here
made of slow, steady hoof-splashes,
                              light, driving rain,
                                    gusting wind.
The forest as rain starts.

Animals scurry,
Straight timbers bend in the gusts,
and creak a little.
Their deep green turns needle-hanging droplets into emeralds
that fit the rich mood.

Lead-gray sky so heavy and low that treetops
gash it.

And sometimes you ride through an even lower cloud . . .
come out . . .
and even the gray-green world seems clear.

Now think autumn . . .
The bluer sky and deeper shadows,
flaming colors and rustling leaves,
sharper, stronger air.
The earth renewing itself,
and you.

Finally, put yourself in winter, in a gentle snowfall . . .
No weight at all
to powdery snow;
it just sifts down
on everything,
and usually stays there
because gravity can hardly pull on it,
it's so light.

When shovels pick it up easily,
the sidewalk is dry underneath.

It won't be snowballs or snowmen.

At night it sparkles.

Think about the beauty of this earth . . .
think from macro to micro, from very big to very small . . .
The beauty of one sky,
       of one ocean,
       of one mountain range,
       of one mountain,
       of one valley,
       of one field,
       of one tree,
       of one limb,
       of one leaf.
The beauty of each overwhelms and humbles.

Most poetry about nature
           is poetry about joy.
Most poetry about the body
           is poetry about joy.

When the two work together
within the oxygen of well-exercised agency,
Joy 1 is the inevitable result.

Bodies

It was May in Teton Park, and winter
was just starting to give way.

Little one-day creeks and streams opened up
                      the snow banks
and cascaded toward the thawing lake.

I was a little like the day . . . it was the early spring
                     of a head cold.
I'd had stuffed sinuses and a hurt-to-swallow throat
for a week,
but that day my head seemed to open up
                     like the scene around me.

I had been alone all day,
going where the road went,
stopping and wandering when I wanted to see something
closer.

I had felt a simple, basic kind of joy
        as I watched a red fox trip-track lightly
        across the frozen lake . . .
        as I saw a Canadian goose straighten his
        neck and pull up out of his dive
        when he saw no open water . . .
        as I felt the strength return to my body . . .
        as I heard and smelled and tasted nature . . .
        as I jogged along a ridge and felt
        the stretch of my legs.

I was vaguely aware that I appreciated the spring
more
because it had been winter; and that I appreciated health
more
because I had been sick.

How ironic that most Christian theology
views the body as a curse . . .
                    a cumbersome, frail, hobbling nuisance
                    that not only limits
                    our movement
                    and our happiness,
                    but is also the root of all that is
                    carnal, and devilish, and bad.

There is no doctrine that is more false,
more opposite from the truth,
than this.

Our bodies are part of the vehicle of joy.

It is true that they are imperfect,
subject to pain
and difficulty and death,
but it is also true that they
allow us to learn things that
we otherwise could not . . .
and that they make us more like God . . .
and that they can ultimately become perfected as his body is.

The spirit needs the element to experience
full sensation and full emotion,
and it will be through the *final* uniting
of spirit and resurrected element
that a fullness of joy will come (D&C 93:33).

Think for a moment about the wonder of our present
"imperfect" bodies.

Think about the difference in efficiency between the heart
and any man-made pump.
Think about the difference in durability between the lungs
and any man-made bellows.

The fascination of science with the body grows and grows
as man learns more and more
about the width of the gap between
            man's technology and God's.

Think about the joys inherent in the body.

Have you felt the joy of finely tuned muscles
working hard,
testing and stretching themselves,
coordinating their movements to fit the nature of the task?

Have you felt the simple joy of
satisfying a body's appetite,
of smelling and eating good basic food when really hungry,
of a hot shower after a long, cold day?

Have you felt the joy of rhythm and dance,
of letting your body express the music its ears hear?

How acutely have you felt the joy
of each of your senses? Have you felt joy
in the simple scent of a sea breeze,
or the touch of a polished stone,
or the sound of a distant woodpecker?

Have you ever sensed all five senses at once . . .
and appreciated the senses themselves,
            as well as the things they were sensing?

I saw an expensive new camera advertised:
            "wide angle lens
            no flash needed indoors
            develops pictures in 20 seconds
            true color reproduction . . ."
each quality vastly inferior to the incredible camera
of the eye . . .

And men are probably even further from
anything comparable
to the intricate sound receptor of the ear,
or the microscopic magic of one tiny taste bud,
or the continuous antenna of the skin,
or the vast scent discrimination of the nose.

All the joys of the senses can exist in nature
or
on a busy Manhattan street . . .
where one man experiences only irritation
                                    and exasperation
while another man, a more alive man,
hears enough to notice the music
that is in the traffic and commotion
        as he walks from his bus to his building . . .
feels enough to notice people (not obstructions)
waiting to get on his elevator
        (and he even helps an old one get on) . . .
sees enough to notice that Central Park
from his way-up window
is a great green rectangle,
sunken, and
with blue patches; its straight gray walls
serving double as the walls of skyscrapers,
one of which he sits in.
The second man notices things through his senses that
the first man misses.
The second man feels joy that
the first man misses.
It is Joy 1.

We are often almost afraid of our senses . . .
afraid that too much joy and too much enjoyment
of the earth
is somehow not pleasing to God.

In fact,
it is too little joy that stops our progress
and displeases our Father.

Just as no one was ever condemned for having too much love,
so also
no one will ever be condemned for having too much joy.

The joy of the body is external through the senses,
but it is also internal
through the exquisite functioning of the body itself.

My father-in-law lived healthy and strong for 89 years,
a farmer who worked hard every day
and loved that work enough to give it the credit
for his extended health and vigor.

We loaded hay bales together one day, he and I,
just a few years before his death,
and when I asked him why he supposed it was
that I got tired before he did,
he took it as a serious question and said
        he guessed it was because I didn't enjoy the work
        as much as he did.

He said he thought the greatest joy was in work.
He said he thought there were two kinds of tired . . .
        the bad kind, born of frustration,
        which makes a man complain and feel abused,
        and the good kind, born of hard, purposeful work,
        which makes a man relax while he toils,
        and feel grateful while he aches.

What he said made me think of something
George Bernard Shaw wrote:
>"This is the true joy in life,
>the being used for a purpose recognized by yourself
>as a mighty one;
>the being thoroughly worn out
>before you are thrown on the scrap heap;
>the being a force of Nature
>instead of a feverish selfish little clod
>of ailments and grievances complaining that
>the world will not devote itself to
>making you happy."[1]

One illustration of how important our bodies are,
of how much they affect our moods and our happiness,
is the fact that we speak of emotions
in bodily terms:
>"Keep your chin up."
>"He has guts."
>"Keep a stiff upper lip."
>"Grit your teeth."
>"Lost your head."
>"Pain in the neck."
>"Hard-nosed."
>etc.

Our bodies are the receptors,
our senses the antennae through which
we experience our world.

Just as radio signals need a receiver,
so the emotions of this life need a body . . .
both to send
and to receive.

---

1. *Man and Superman* (New York: Dodd, Mead & Company, 1931), pp. xxxiv-xxxv.

Some theories of joy would have us believe
that we have to "get out of our bodies"
to feel real ecstasy . . .
that only when we somehow transcend the physical
and totally lose ourselves,
and become "swallowed up" by some outside presence
(thus forgetting and becoming unaware of our bodies),
only then,
they say,
are we able to feel real joy.

Actually, just the opposite is true.
Full joy is felt when we are *most* aware of our bodies.

In moments of spirituality and great inspiration
people are not less but more aware
of all that is around them
and of their bodies themselves.

The derivative words of *ecstasy* are
"stand out,"
not "swallowed up."

Joseph Smith was intensely and acutely aware of his own body
during his first vision.
We know this because he described so vividly his physical feelings
and temporal sensations.

Agency

The third indispensable part
of our second estate,
and thus
an indispensable part of Joy 1,
is our agency . . . our freedom of choice . . . the key

element in the preexistent plan
we each voted to follow.
It is hard to fully appreciate this agency,
because we know and remember nothing else.

We can only imagine the contrast of the plan we know
with the plan that Satan put forward.
His was one of coercion,
        one of force,
        one of tyranny,
        one void of alternatives or choice.

Some earthly situations simulate that plan, and
give us insights into the horror
of what he proposed.

Imagine a war captive, in a cell,
with no physical freedom,
brain-washed and mind-controlled to the point
        of not knowing who he is . . . whipped into submission
        by men intent on taking away his will and his agency
        to further their own power.

Even this stark picture,
in reality,
is nothing like what Satan's plan would have brought about.

The man in the cell still has the positive options
        of trying to keep control of his mind,
        of trying not to hate his persecutors,
        of trying somehow to escape,
        of hoping against hope for rescue.

And he has the negative options
        of dying,
        of quitting,
        of giving in to his bitterness and hate.

Had we come to earth without agency,
there would have been no positive or negative options
because there would have been no positive or negative.
And the total tyranny of that
is probably not even possible
                    for us to conceive.

The joy of agency is the joy of choice.
Joy is present in a thing we do out of choice,
and not present when we do that *same* thing
                    by force and without choice.

If you *choose* to climb a mountain,
there is exhilaration and fulfillment at the top.
If you are *forced* to climb it,
the top is made of pain and fatigue.

A book read by choice is far more interesting
than the same book read by assignment.

There is no ultimate coercion on this earth . . .
humans cannot totally take away the options
of other humans.
Thus all have agency,
and the very existence of that agency produces
                    a certain level of joy.

Agency, however, should not be confused with freedom.
Freedom results from truth and intelligence,
from knowledge of and obedience to
the laws of God and of the universe.
Freedom must be learned,
and earned.

I'm free to jump because I know
the sequence of muscle contractions that produces
                    a spring into the air . . .
but I'm not free to levitate
because I don't know the law that would allow me to
stay up there after I've jumped.

I'm free to drive to California because I know
                    how to drive a car, and
                    how to buy gas, and
                    how to get there . . .
but I'm not free to *think* myself instantly there
because I don't know the law that permits it.

Freedom and agency are two different things . . .
one we have to learn and earn,
the other is a gift
(one that we worked and fought for in an earlier sphere).

The truth makes us free
because truth is the tool by which we operate eternal law.
And while we may not possess the truth on this earth
that enables thought transportation or levitation,
we do have available to us
(through earthly and through inspirational sources)
the truth necessary . . . *all* the truth necessary . . .
          to graduate from this earth
                    into a higher grade where higher laws
                    will certainly be taught.

Part of agency
(perhaps an equal half)
is challenge, difficulty, problems . . .

When a man says, "I didn't want these problems . . . I didn't
choose to have these difficulties . . . "
he is wrong.
He did choose them . . . in the preexistence. He chose
to have problems, to face tough decisions,
and to do it all without the mental apron-strings
of preexistent memory.

It is the problems that make the test valid.
Kites rise *against* the wind . . .

The veil
that blocks our memory of the preexistence
is an essential part of our second estate
                              and of our agency.

A part of our second estate because it permits
a test
(an honest test because we can't see the answers).
A part of our agency because in its absence
we would have no agency
(for our choices would already be made).

The veil that gives us agency
is analogous to what science calls a "selective membrane,"
which lets some things in and holds other things out.

The veil holds out our mental memories
            but it lets in the familiarity of spiritual feelings.

We can't remember the preexistence
but, under proper circumstances,
we *can* remember the feeling of the spirit that was there.

That is why a strong testimony of the gospel
provokes a feeling that is somehow familiar,
and that is why spiritual knowledge
carries a "ring of truth."

Perhaps it is this "spiritual recall,"
this subconscious memory of spiritual feeling,
that causes us to exult in the joy of nature.
Perhaps the joy that we felt in the preexistence as
we saw the earth being created *for us*
somehow lingers with us and comes out
as we become a part
of what we saw.

Joy comes through the exercise of faith (Philippians 1:25).
Faith can exist only in the absence of complete knowledge . . .
an absence which the veil brings about.

I remember a midterm exam
in my most difficult class.
I had studied harder than ever before.
My friend knew the course . . . it was his major . . .
he didn't have to study.
We both got A's on the exam.
His meant little, mine meant much.

The joy of faith is the joy of
making it on your own . . .
doing it without being forced . . .
finding the answer that is not given.

Just as any material thing is worth more
when it is earned
and sacrificed for,
so also our actions and the things we achieve
are worth more when done by faith
than when done under coercion or by perfect knowledge.

40

One reason that there will be ultimate joy
in salvation
is that those who receive it will have
"worked out their own salvation."
This true achievement
will bring true joy.

The other necessary element in salvation
(the one needed in addition to works)
is grace . . .
the gift of God . . . the atonement of Christ.

One thing we should treasure even more
than something we have earned and sacrificed for
is something that *someone else* has sacrificed for . . .
something given in complete love.

Thus salvation is the greatest of all joys
because
it comes only by works *and* by grace,
and is both
earned by ourselves and given by Christ.

It is sacrifice that gives worth to possessions,
and salvation comes only through
our sacrifice
and the ultimate sacrifice of our elder Brother.

But now, you see, we are getting into
achievements
and relationships,
and they are well beyond the stuff of Joy 1
and should be reserved for chapters to come.

Joy 1—Overview

I met a Hawaiian once who was the embodiment of Joy 1.
He was not the Waikiki variety, but a true Hawaiian
who lived on the more primitive "Big Island."

He picked me up in his old car.
(I was hitchhiking.)
He asked where I was going
       and drove me all the way there.
       (It took eight hours.)
He wore only a faded pair of trunks.
He showed me his favorite trees on the way . . .
he explained everything to me with great animation
                          and interest,
almost as though he were seeing it for the first time himself . . .
from the waterfalls to the flowers,
from the lava flows to the rain forests,
from how the trade winds caused the sudden, dry deserts
       to how his feet had become hard enough not to need shoes.

He said his name was Rusty.
He was uneducated but he had great knowledge.
He was penniless but not poor.
His grammar was weak but his voice was powerful.
Other than his old car, he had no possessions,
              but he owned the earth.

In some ways he was the happiest man I've ever met.

When we got to my destination, I said how lucky I felt
that he had happened to be going where I was going.
He said: "Oh. . . . no . . .
       I was only going to the grocery store
       down the street.
       But I can do that tomorrow.

I couldn't give you a ride tomorrow . . .
                so I did it today."
He was childlike in his joy,
in his spontaneous delight.

I kept asking myself if his joy was born of his
carefree existence and lack of responsibility.

I kept wondering if someone in a faster-paced world,
with more responsibility,
could feel the same joy.

I kept getting the feeling
that there was some connection
between Rusty's joy
and Christ's admonition to all of us to
"become as little children" (Matthew 18:3).

As with all of Christ's words, these four are
better understood
not in the context of harsh admonition or
                         arbitrary command,
but in the context of loving counsel from a
wise elder Brother
who *wants* us to have joy
and is telling us *how*.

One incredible thing about Joy 1
is that generally we are born with it and then
gradually
lose it . . . give it up . . . forget what it is and
how to have it.

If you want a demonstration of Joy 1,
watch a child.

I watched one one day . . .
my own . . . in our yard . . .
a two-year-old.
I watched her (unobserved) for exactly fifteen minutes.

It had rained the night before and she was
interested in how the little droplets
left each leaf to run down her finger
as she reached up and touched them from below.

She tried it ten times, once with each finger
                                        and thumb,
and giggled out loud when
the accumulated drops gained enough weight to run
down her arm and drip off her elbow.

Then a small stone caught the morning sun and
                                        attracted her eye.
She picked it up, turned it over and over, and then
lifted up her smock and tried to fit it
into the hollow of her "belly button."

It was too big, so she tossed it aside.
It bounced across the brick patio and made a
hollow, ringing sound.
Delighted, she picked it up and threw it again, listening . . .
six or seven more times . . .
                                        and would have continued . . .
but a tiny sparrow folded its wings
and glided onto the peg of our birdhouse,
                                        above her head.

She turned her face up and said
"Hi bird!"
(She had said "Hi!" to the sky and the grass and the bush
when she came out,
and she usually said "goodbye" when she went in.)

Then she climbed into the swing I had made for her . . .
and the joy in her face was as evident
as the wind in her hair.

My little girl, in a few moments, had demonstrated
a great awareness
of her body and of its sensations,
of nature and all of her surroundings,
and of the freedom to act with and in the physical world.

She had demonstrated Joy 1 . . . by simply receiving it,
active, invigorating, spontaneous delight.

All young children demonstrate it
unless they are sick or hungry,
or unless some grown-up snuffs it out somehow.

If only we could learn it from them . . .
and preserve it in them . . .

We know
that our second estate is the vehicle for joy . . .
that our *bodies* are not a curse and a limitation
        but a blessing and an extension
                of what we were before . . .
that the *world* is not a hell
                but a heaven in embryo . . .
that our *agency* is not a license to abuse and destroy
                but an opportunity to grow and progress.

Together these give us the potential for Joy 1 . . .
for pleasure . . .
for the physical enjoyments.
Together they are the vehicle
which is a joy in and of itself
and which is the necessary prerequisite of all
higher levels of joy.

4

The Pursuit of Joy 1

When mail delivery was dependent on stagecoaches
and the Pony Express,
      it was also dependent
on Indians, washed-out roads, sick horses, broken
                          wagon-wheels,
and any other thing that might affect
the condition
of the vehicle by which the mail was carried.

If Joy 1 is dependent on the *vehicle*
of our bodies,
and our earth,
and our agency,
then it is also dependent on the condition
                    of all three.

Joy 1 is the joy derived directly from the vehicle.
Joy 1 is pursued by maximizing
the condition and the functioning of the vehicle.

If you want to maximize the functioning of your car,
you have to consider the condition of three things:

1. The body of the vehicle (the exterior and interior)
2. The drive of the vehicle (the engine and transmission)
3. The environment of the vehicle (the road you are on)

If you want to maximize the functioning
of the vehicle of joy,
you must consider the same three conditions:

1. Of the body (your body, exterior and interior)

2. Of the drive (your agency and
                    how you use it)
3. Of the environment (the earth)

The extent to which each is enhanced, extended, expanded,
magnified, maximized,
improved, increased
determines the extent of Joy 1.

How do we increase the joy of our bodies?
How do we increase the joy of our agency?
How do we increase the joy of this earth?

One answer works for all three questions.
The same sequence of steps improves each of the three.

We increase the joy of *body, agency,* and *earth*
1. by awareness and appreciation.
2. by use and maintenance.
3. by discipline.

Appreciation and Awareness

Our *bodies* are improved, our *earth* enhanced, and our *agency*
increased
        by appreciation and awareness.

As mentioned earlier, our senses improve
        as we are more aware of them . . .
Consider the blind man who hears so much more because
he doesn't see.
Consider the difference in the taste of food
before and after a fast.

We use our senses at about ten percent of capability.
Capacity increases as conscious use increases.

Senses are the windows
between our minds
and the rest of the world.
The mind controls the size of the window
and pulls the drapes back so that full light can come through.

So the message is awareness . . .
See something new on your old route tomorrow . . .
Separate individual sounds out of the noise of each day . . .
Smell and touch the lilacs you walk past,
                                        instead of just looking . . .
See if your taste can identify the ingredients in your food.

Stand in nature and block all but one sense.
First just see.
Then just hear.
Then just smell.
Then just taste.
Then just feel. Then
open all five into their
synchronized sensual symphony.

It is awareness and appreciation of our individual and particular
gifts
(and of their uniqueness)
that causes us to develop and perfect them,
and that brings into synchronicity
our agency and our ability,
effectively coupling our choices with our capacity.

All have talents and unique attributes,
though one person's may be more obvious
                                        than another's.

Discovering and using these gifts produces joy.
Coveting the gifts of others causes grief.

As Emerson said:
"Envy is ignorance, and imitation is suicide."

I believe he meant the second part
very literally.
If you copy someone, you are ending
yourself
through lack of use.

Individuality is beauty and
uniqueness is life.

Be aware and appreciative of choices . . .
(alternatives, options, and forks in the road)
thus building the joy of agency
(options don't exist until we're aware of them).
Then pick the path unique to you
(where your choice is well coupled with your capacity).

I thought about uniqueness as I
drove through a high mountain pass and noticed
the graphic pattern of the lodge-pole pines
as I whispered by in my car.
My eyes got rapid-fire multiple snapshots
of straight, parallel trunks
with dark green backdrop behind.

Here and there the vertical parallel pattern
and the brown-green colors
were spattered
by the crooked trunks and ash white
of aspen trees.

Each aspen was outnumbered one thousand to one.
Each dared to have a white trunk while all others around were
brown.
Each dared to curve and bend while all others stood rigid.
Each dared to wear silver-dollar round leaves
        while all others around wore traditional needles.

We all need to learn how to
follow the drummer we hear . . . and how
(in partnership with the Lord) to set our own course.

This earth is also improved by appreciation and awareness.

Some claim that nature itself—even house plants
respond to appreciation . . .
and it is our awareness that causes us
        to take care of the earth . . .
        to strive to make it a better place to live in.

All the earth and all that is on it are lessons for study
in the great school of our Heavenly Father.

We should be able to appreciate the earth
simply by virtue of the many things we have in common with it.
We say "Mother Earth" because we are, in so many ways,
born
of this earth
and because we experience so many of the
same things
that the earth does.

The earth was created by God.
The earth was baptized.
The earth will be sanctified and purified and celestialized.

We often hear the admonition
        "Be in the world but not of the world,"
and we take only the second part as an admonition.
How about the first? "Be in the world."
Is that not also an admonition?
We must be in the world before we can affect the world,
and we are in the world only if we are a part of it,
                only if we understand it,
                only if we appreciate it.

Use and Maintenance

It is interesting to note
the opposite nature
of man-made things and God-made things.
Use wears out man-made things
                but *strengthens* God-made things.

Any talent *improves* with practice . . .
any muscle *grows* with use . . .

We sometimes understand only part of that law.
We know that our biceps will enlarge if we exercise them
over and over,
day after day . . .
But few realize that
their eyesight,
or their sense of smell,
or their hearing
will also improve and expand
with proper and positive use.
As will their talents.

Use your skills and gifts.
Like the talents in the parable, the important thing
is not how many you start with
(or what they are) . . .
What is important is only what you do with them
(and what they become).

When you use a talent . . . when you perform in any way . . .
do it not to boast or to elevate yourself.
Rather,
do it to glorify the Lord . . . to demonstrate to him your
gratitude for the gift he gave you.
This one attitude differential
will make your performance
inspiring rather than boastful,
magnanimous rather than conceited, and will promote
admiration and love rather than jealousy and envy.

Use your body to repent with.
A prophet has said that one very important reason
for a body
is that it is a vehicle through which
we can overcome inadequacies that are somehow harder
to purge out when we have only our spiritual bodies . . . [1]
Such repentance is apparently terribly difficult
when we have no body to do it with.

While we do not fully understand it,
we know that our physical bodies and our temporal earth
somehow give us a special escalated ability to learn and grow
as they accentuate our chance to experience.

---

1. Melvin J. Ballard, "Three Degrees of Glory," in Bryant S. Hinckley, *Sermons and Missionary Services of Melvin J. Ballard* (Deseret Book, 1949), p. 241.

Therefore, to take advantage, we must learn all we can,
                    develop all we can,
                    use our gifts all we can,
                    experience all we can,
for we have only two places in which to prepare for
judgment day . . .
and we know not what our limitations will be
in the spirit world to come.

Like our muscles and our talents, our agency expands with use
and atrophies with idleness or neglect.
We exercise our agency by looking for alternatives and options,
by getting out of ruts and comfort zones
and exploring new places and new ideas,
by trying new things.

Use has an opposite effect
on man-made things and on God-made things,
but *maintenance*
has a similar beneficial effect on each.

Just as one who fails to tune his engine
robs the performance of his vehicle,
so those who fail to tune their bodies, their agency, and their use of
earth
rob themselves of the full potential of Joy 1.

Most know the difference between drudgery,
sawing with a dull saw,
and the elation and exhilaration of the crisp cutting
of a shiny, sharpened one.

Use and maintain your body.
"Work out"
could have triple meaning.
1. *Work out* as in exercise
to maximize both the function and joy of body.
2. As you exercise, it will help you sort out,
purge out, and *work out* stress and confusion.
3. *"Working out"* your own salvation:
both the exercise and the mental sorting are important parts.

Use and maintain your agency.
If you don't define and make choices,
they will define and make you.
We become better decision-makers
by practice!

Use and maintain the earth.
What if the first question on judgment day is,
"Why didn't you use those mountains I made for you?
or experience that sea coast or go to that desert?
Didn't you understand they were there for you to enjoy?"

Discipline

Discipline is the cap
that keeps our celebration and use of the physical
from overflowing and carrying us away.
Discipline opens and closes the right doors,
starts us and stops us at the right times,
gets us up when we should but keeps us
from staying up too long,
gets us to eat and exercise enough
but not too much.

Discipline applied to agency
circles the parameters of acceptable alternatives,
shutting out the dangerous and the damaging,
the offensive, obsessive, and obscene,
so we choose from among the goods.

The earth has its own discipline
from its sunrises to its tides
and needs from us only our discipline of its use.
So we tread lightly,
putting back more than we take out.
We should respect it as our teacher.
Brigham Young said:

> "The earth is very good in and of itself,
> and has abided a celestial law.
> Consequently we should not despise it,
> nor desire to leave it, but rather strive to obey
> the same law
> that the earth abides."[2]

One defining difference
between animals (the creations of God)
and people (the offspring of God)
is that animals fulfill the measure of their creation
by following their instincts and satisfying their appetites
while we fulfill our measure
by refining our instincts
and controlling our appetites.

---

2. *Journal of Discourses,* 2:302–303.

Most animals
eat ravenously to satisfy their hunger,
mate indiscriminately, obeying every urge,
migrate instinctively
by season or to follow the herd.
Always there is an animalistic satisfaction,
never is there joy.

For God's children,
purpose is fulfilled and Joy 1 realized and maximized
with the discipline and personal governance
of each appetite.
Eat more selectively, less, slower,
taste and appreciate food.

Handle all other appetites similarly.
Control the urges that would otherwise control you.
Christ lived and taught the mastery of appetites,
and "discipline" is a derivative
of "disciple."

Pursuit of Joy 1—Overview

Since we are quoting Brigham Young . . .
he summarized the basic fact of our relationship to this earth
and to all of our second estate:
> "Whatever you have, it is the Lord's.
> You own nothing."[3]
> "If I have horses, oxen, and possessions,
> they are the Lord's and not mine;
> and all I ask is for him to tell me
> what to do with them."[4]

And so it is with all of our
second estate . . .

---

3. *Journal of Discourses,* 10:298.
4. *Journal of Discourses,* 6:46.

We are stewards over our bodies,
                over our earth,
                over our agency.

How well we handle this stewardship
will determine
whether we will ever have *ownership*
over any of the three.

There is a circular, self-momentum-sustaining
spiral
involved in the pursuit of Joy 1.

Appreciation and use and discipline
of body, earth, and agency create Joy 1,
and then the very feeling and presence of Joy 1
further expands the senses . . .
        we see more and feel more and hear more . . .
and thus Joy 1 spirals, increases, and expands further . . .

More appreciation,
use, and discipline
of body, earth,
and agency

More Joy 1

bringing still more awareness, use, and discipline

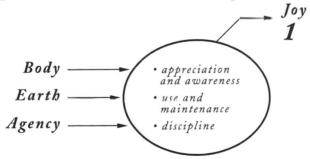

Joy
1

Body ⟶ • *appreciation*
            and awareness

Earth ⟶ • *use and*
            maintenance

Agency ⟶ • *discipline*

and expanding our potential to create for ourselves Joy 2.

5

The Enhancers or Prompters of Joy
Relationships and Achievements

1. The Vehicle of Joy
Our second estate—
earth, bodies, agency
(physical)

2. The Enhancers or Prompters
Relationships and
accomplishments
(social/emotional)

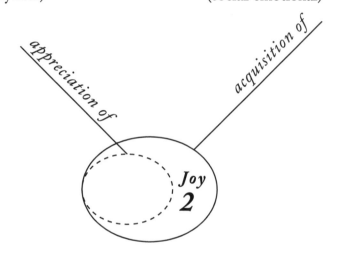

Six Stories: Part Two

Turn back to pages 21–24
to remember part one of each story.

"The Flower and the Camera"—Part Two

Since the flower is near your front door
you notice it each day, going and coming.

You see its growth and changes and feel with it
a relationship.
One day it is so particularly beautiful that
you get your camera
and achieve a spectacular, close-focus picture of it.
Your small, flower-joy is enhanced.
(to be continued)

"The First Lawn Mowing"—Part Two

The camaraderie of doing it together,
the rapport with Mom that brought about the idea,
and the love for Dad that makes them smile
       when they think about what he'll say
          when he sees it . . .
these relationships and the basic achievement of having *done* it
turn Joy 1 into Joy 2.
(to be continued)

"The Love Story"—Part Two

As months passed, they learned the mental
and emotional tenderness of love.
They could talk fully and deeply and freely about all things.
They had no secrets from each other.
They made commitments, one of which was marriage.
They could communicate with words or with touch
or simply by looking into each other's eyes.
They became close enough
that each could know the other's needs and moods
and thoughts.
Together they dreamed dreams,
together they generated ideas,
together they formulated goals,
together they shared Joy 2.
(to be continued)

"The Marriage"—Part Two

As they look across the altar,
her eyes tell his
that what he feels, she shares.
A relationship so close to oneness that
                              words are hardly needed.
After the proposal and their engagement
a commitment had come about
which took all of the taking out of the relationship
and made it a contest of out-giving each other.
It was a relationship of giving
and today it was becoming one of covenant.
The relationship was warmed and calmed
by respect, both for self and for each other.

Each had done well in school;
he had finished, she was about to.
Each felt the fulfillment of achievement
and the positive satisfaction of past and anticipated success.
(to be continued)

"The New Arrival"—Part Two

You reflect on the nervous husband who made you
sit down
for the whole first days after you told him you were
pregnant . . .
He stood by, close by. It was an experience
for two, then three . . . not for one, then two.
The love in that current *relationship* and . . .
the current *achievement* in converting the den to a nursery.
The anticipation of a *relationship* with a child
(his dreams of a baseball and two mitts in the backyard
and hers of ballet slippers and pigtails and junior proms) . . .
The anticipation of the *achievement* of raising
the child properly . . .

All these add up to another level of joy
where emotional and social elements are added to
the physical,
where relationships and achievements
become the prompters of Joy 2.
(to be continued)

"The Promotion"—Part Two

The letter is a promotion, and with it comes
The corner executive suite,
The payoff for twenty-five years of hard work,
The achievement of a goal,
The realization of recognition,
The rekindled belief that his life might make a difference.
(to be continued)

Glimpses of Joy 2

Imagine sitting one night, you and I and others,
in a fireside group.
There are fifteen of us, some married, all friends in the gospel.
It is a soft, mellow evening in autumn,
and there is a mood of openness and sharing
that seems to fit the evening's topic.
The topic is joy.

We are each asked to recall some moment from our lives
when we were consciously aware of joy,
some specific moment, well fixed in place and in time,
when we had felt real joy . . . joy that we could explain
and describe.

Then, in turn, we are each asked to relate our moment.
From these expressions we hope to be able to find some
similar threads,

some points of commonality that we can define
as the *elements* or *components* of joy.
Some of the responses are predictable . . .
others come as complete surprises . . .
yet all the responses have certain similarities,
certain *kindred elements.*

Kirstin is first, and she
describes the birth of her first child;
and it is her description
that makes up the story "The New Arrival"
contained in chapters three, five, seven, and nine
of this book.

Her husband, Howard, is next.
He says his first-impression-response
(we've been asked for first impressions)
was his law-school graduation.
To him it represented the long-awaited culmination
of years of work,
and he says the satisfaction of standing atop the peak
that he had looked up at for so long
was true joy.

Robyn and Joshua, the next couple,
have independently each thought of the same joy.
Together, they describe the experience of a year earlier
when their small son
had undergone major surgery . . .
when both his life and his potential to live normally
had hung in the balance.
Their fear of the worst magnified the joy in
the doctor's post-operative announcement that all was well.
His words were, to them, a glowing message
of the greatest joy they had ever heard.

Norm, sitting next in the circle,
expresses a somewhat simpler joy.
On his farm, he says, each spring on that certain day
when the ground has finally become warm enough
to plow . . .
and when the first furrow is opened and when
the fresh seeds slip out of sight into
the deep, black earth . . .
when the miracle begins that leads to harvest in the fall . . .
"on that plough day," he says, "each year . . . I feel joy."

His wife, Patti, smiles and says she knew
Norm would say that.
Then she tells how, when she was only fourteen,
her quilt won the blue ribbon at the county fair.
Before that day she had been a forlorn, dejected teenager . . .
left out of one group because of her old clothes,
rejected by another because she wouldn't smoke . . .
unwanted, unappreciated, sorry for herself.
After the quilt,
she felt worth . . . she felt importance.
She had a destiny after that . . . an identity and a uniqueness
she could be proud of,
and she liked herself because of that one thing
at which she was best.

Kelly says her first thought was of her
Primary class . . .
the four-year-olds with their angelic faces and their eyes
that light like candles when they understand.
Kelly says that giving to them and receiving from them . . .
kneading their open minds with useful and eternal truths . . .
brings out the best in her.
And she says that seeing their spontaneous delight,
their open, overt love,

their realness and candor,
rekindles the same qualities inside of her and allows
their joy to become hers.

Bill's joy is a particular
momentary instant of emotion when he,
after a two-week vacation, returned to his daughters
(ages three and four . . . left with the grandparents).
Two little sets of arms around his neck and the words
"I love you, Daddy . . . we missed you."
Bill says that the joy of that simple reunion
was as strong and as vibrant as any joy he has ever felt.

Chuck is next.
He's almost apologetic for his;
it goes back so far and seems so trivial that he hesitates
to mention it. . . . He is from England and
he says he remembers the day his
high school team won the soccer championship.
The feeling was more closeness than wild ecstasy,
                    more loyalty than celebration,
                    more brotherhood than conquest.
He remembers the joy of friendship
and of the process of achieving a teamwork goal.

Emily recalls the night when she made
her decision
about going to medical school.
She remembers that decision as the culmination of an
extensive process of soul-searching, of deciding
on priorities,
and of ranking and categorizing her objectives and interests.
She says that the settled, sure, clear feeling that covered her
like a blanket
once that decision was made
was a solid, tangible taste of real joy.

Bernard conducts the metropolitan symphony,
and his answer comes quickly because
the very night before
they had played the opening concert of the season,
and Bernard was still feeling the exhilaration
of the experience.
He says that hearing those soft strings and booming percussions
rise and fall to meet the movement and command of his hands
created joy.
He says that feeling the audience's satisfaction
with what he had worked so long to build
brought his joy.

Loraine's happiness was easy to describe.
Her joy was the joy that she felt in Bernard's joy.
It was his joy of being happy because the one she loved
more than herself was happy.

Peter, Bernard's friend, and the composer of some
of the music that Bernard had performed the night before
has a specific recollection of one night, trying to write
a major movement
of an original sonata . . .
a moment when, without explanation, notes flowed from
his pen to the page.
As if guided by some unseen hand, they
fell into place and onto the page with such precision
and cadence
that he had a hard time recognizing the finished product
as his own work.
He says that the inspirational process of
brilliant flashes of creativity was,
to him,
sublime and supreme joy.

Helga is next to last in the circle.
She says that her thought response to the joy question
jumped into her mind as a surprise . . .
but held its place there above the
more common joy memories that tried to follow.
Her first thought was of her last Thursday, spent
in a genealogical library.
She says that the unexpected discovery of a whole line
of her father's ancestors
gave her a sudden extension of identity . . .
and with it a genuine feeling of joy.

You're next, you're last in the circle.
What specific moment of joy
comes first to your mind?

Now, if you will recall,
the preannounced objective of our fireside
was to discover the elements common to all joy . . .
     to see if there were particular
     components
     that always
     went into the make-up of joy.

The joy stories have taken over two hours, and with each
passing minute the conclusion has become more obvious . . .
     All joy . . .
     every single response . . .
     centers around
         a *relationship*
         or an *achievement.*

In each and every case,
it was the interest or
      the fulfillment or
      the excitement or
      the emotion of
a relationship or of an achievement
           that *prompted* and ignited the joy.

Kirstin's relationship with her child,
Howard's achievement in finishing law school,
Kelly's relationship with her Primary children,
Bernard's achievement in conducting the symphony,
and so on.

Let's look slightly deeper into the two enhancers or prompters of
joy . . .
first into relationships
and then into achievements.

Relationships

I sat on the 767 as it sped down the runway
and watched
horizontal drops stream across
the rounded pane
as the jet pulled up its wet wheels
and flew.

First there was only solid grey there,
pressing in tight
on the glass.

Then gradually
lighter grey . . . then wispy white
going by.

Suddenly a burst-quick of blue,
and another . . .
filmy white traces zipping by.

Then all at once we burst through
into the morning-blue sky . . .
skimming the top billows of clouds that were
brilliant white
in the newly present sun.

I almost felt guilty for taking the time to notice the beauty
of the takeoff
because there was a memo
I had to write
before I landed.
As I got started on it, the man in the next seat
said, "Hello," and asked me how I was.

I said, "Fine,"
and went right back to the memo.
He tried twice more to start up a conversation,
        and I ended the effort twice more with one-word,
        terminal answers.

Later that night I lay in bed and thought back.
The memo was done, but the man was gone.
The chance of any relationship with him was past.

I tried to rationalize my thought with the notion
that I had never seen that man
before,
and would likely never see him again . . . so why, I thought,
should I worry?

I then had the disconcerting realization
that,
to one who believes the restored gospel's concept
of preexistence and of hereafter,
there can never be a meeting wherein one is *sure*
that he has never met the person before
or
that he will never meet him again.

I had traded the possibility of an emotional, eternal asset
(a friendship)
       for a temporary, temporal one (a memo).

Too strong an orientation to *things*
can shut out *relationships* . . .
can cause us to build walls instead of bridges.

Relationships are the essence of beauty and of experience.
If there is anything more beautiful than
nature,
it is a relationship with nature.
If there is anything more beautiful than a person,
it is a relationship with a person.

While it is true that any relationship
(even a ten-minute one on a plane)
is potentially an asset of eternal duration,
it is also true that the greater joy, the truest joy of relationships,
comes not in the superficial or the shallow
but in the total and the deep.

Tillich spoke of the joy of the things that are deep:

"Eternal joy is not to be reached
by living on the surface. It is
rather attained by breaking through
the surface, by penetrating the
deep things of ourselves, of our world,
and of God."[1]

Linda and I,
in the days of our courtship,
dated on two different levels . . .
first on a social, surface level
of fun without commitment . . .
of light talk and the simple enjoyment of being together
and of sharing our time with each other.
Later we dated on a deeper, more emotional level
of oneness and love and growing commitment . . .
of sharing our secrets and our souls.

I remember the specific night
when the *transition* from shallow to deep
took place.
When I went home on that eternally important night,
sleep was far away, so I picked up a pen and wrote these lines:

"Sun's late glow on blue-fading clouds . . .
the evening sky above the
new-green quad,
and later
the misty valley, soft shadows, darker sky . . .

But no wind, no temperature . . .
an equilibrium night of spring, memories, campus . . .
our campus, our memories . . .
and we remembered so much
of hills and Hondas, snow and smiles . . .

---

1. Paul Tillich, *The Shaking of the Foundations* (New York: Charles Scribner's Sons, 1948), p. 63.

But also, last night,
I listened to your eyes, heard your feelings,
felt the confidence and excitement of looking out
at the world when
>your hand is in mine
>>and my thoughts are ours.

Linda,
was I with you again . . . or for the first time?"

In scripture,
there are hundreds of verses where the word *joy* appears.

Try to find even one where the word is not used
in a relationship setting.
You will not be able to. The writers of scripture invariably
compared and related *joy* to *relationships*.

Some of my favorites are:

3 John 1:4: No greater joy than to hear that one's children walk in truth.
Proverbs 23:24: Being the parent of a righteous, wise child brings joy.
2 John 1:12: The joy of communication, of speaking face to face.
1 Thessalonians 3:9: The joy of missionary work.
2 Corinthians 1:24: Missionaries are "helpers of joy" of others.
Acts 20:24: The joy of service and of sacrifice.

Accomplishments

What do the following persons have in common?
The young child after he cleans his room.
The mountain climber who reaches the pinnacle.
The student who aces the test.

The author who finishes his manuscript.
The farmer when his grain is in the barn.
The artist who completes his painting.

They have two things in common.
One is some degree of fatigue, of physical or mental exhaustion;
but *one* is not evident because of *two* . . .
Two is elation—an achievement-exhilaration that melts
away the fatigue
as an oven melts snow.

We are born to achieve, to accomplish, to bring things to pass.
The ability to do so is a gift of this mortality
where we have stewardships
and physical matter on which to act.
We are born to be successful and to
accomplish relevant goals that benefit the world
and that build God's kingdom.
The Lord is the most successful of all beings.
He has achieved more than any other . . .
and he is *still* achieving.
(To say God is omnipotent is not to say
he has accomplished all, for indeed,
to bring us, his children, back to his presence
is an accomplishment that he has told us is
current . . .
it is *now* his work and his glory . . . and his *joy*.)

An interesting distinction between satisfaction and happiness
is that happiness is partially comprised of
not yet being satisfied.

Bertrand Russell said,
"Not having some things you want is
an essential ingredient of happiness."

Striving for what we are still missing
can deepen both
the depth of achievement and the depth of joy.

As in relationships, there is some element
of joy in even the smallest, simplest, most unexpected
achievement.
But as also with relationships, the joy is far deeper
and fuller in a relevant, substantial, contributing achievement.

None can deny the joy that *can* exist
in doing a good, fulfilling job on simple things:
hanging a picture,
washing the car,
balancing the checkbook,
edging the lawn.

But the gulf between these simple joys
and the deeper joy of major accomplishment is wide.

It would seem that the *relevance*
and magnitude
of any achievement can be measured
by two criteria:
1. What it does for others.
2. What it does for you.

If you write a song that uplifts and inspires . . .
If you build a house that protects and benefits your family . . .
If you create a business that employs people
and gives valuable service to others . . .
If you fill a mission that brings truth to seeking souls . . .
the joy you have given others will magnify your own,
and increase the relevance
of the accomplishment.

Likewise, if you graduate from college with honors . . .
If you earn and receive a promotion . . .
If you improve until you win the tennis tournament . . .
If you master the violin . . .
you have become more than
you were
and, because of your growth,
the achievement has relevance.

It is surprising how many
"accomplishments"
do little or nothing for others
or for self
and thus fall to the category of minor, non-relevant achievement.

Joy 2—Overview

It had been trying to rain all day.
The sky was swollen and gray, and so dark that
it had seemed like evening for hours.
The day was beautiful in a moody, thoughtful sort of way.
I was sitting high in a hotel room looking
over the green Potomac River and its greener banks,
working on the manuscript for this book.
     I was working on chapter 10 at the time,
     but I went back and pulled out chapter 5
     because I realized that what I was feeling was Joy 2.

I had nearly completed the manuscript
and I felt the joy of accomplishment . . .
of having worked hard and tried hard
to say things I felt.

I had been away from my family for two days
and had just talked to them on the phone.

The love in their voices was magnified
by the melancholy missing that the heart always feels
        when they seem so close on the phone
        but are so far away.

So I felt the joy of relationships, too ... and
there was some hard-to-describe similarity
between my heart
and the clouds which finally opened
and let the rain spill out.

Relationships and achievements are the enhancers of joy
and the prompters of Joy 2.

They are the two worthy goal categories of life.
Every worthwhile pursuit is a relationship
or a relevant, righteous achievement.

If we believe that,
we need to stop and analyze how much time
we spend on either or both,
because most spend most
of their time and mental energy
on neither.

6

The Pursuit of Joy 2

Joy 2 is the joy that occurs
through the vehicle of joy (second estate)
because of the prompters or enhancers of joy (relationships and
achievements).

One man,
whom I have respected and admired all of my life,
once told me that
the key to happiness
is to have a *cause* . . .
to be always championing a cause of *merit* and *worth*.

Now . . .
if it is true (and it is)
that the two categories of worthwhile things on this earth
are relationships and achievements,
we need to have "achievement causes"
and we need to have "relationship causes."
True happiness requires that we have both
        and that we be effectively
        pursuing both.

Considering the uncountable number of complete books
that have been written on how to relate
        and on how to achieve . . .
can we hope to deal effectively with either in
one chapter?

Perhaps,
because the principles governing relationships and
achievements are very simple . . .
and thus are better discussed simply
        than in extended and complex terms.

Both can be pursued strongly
                    and directly
                    and effectively,
and the principles governing their pursuit
are basically simple.

Each of the two (relationships and achievements)
is pursued
in two principal ways:
          1. Through objectives.
          2. Through attitudes.

The pursuit of both relationships and achievements requires
well-set *goals* and *objectives*
          (although the *type* of goals required is different,
          one from the other).

The pursuit of both relationships and achievements
requires particular *attitudes*
          (although the nature of the attitudes is different,
          one from the other).

Thus there are two major sections of this chapter,
each with two parts.

First, a section on pursuit by objective
          (with a part on relationships and
          a part on achievements).

Second, a section on pursuit by attitude
          (with a part on relationships and
          a part on achievements).

The two combined are a
blueprint
for building Joy 2.

Pursuit by Objective

Once there were four people.
One of them had no goals . . . led an aimless,
purposeless life . . .
and made little of himself and learned little from others
        and did little for others.

The other three had goals.
One of them had the wrong goals.
Her objectives were of the world . . .
she wanted money and power, approval and acclaim.
She wanted pleasure and luxury
        and the envy of others.
She achieved her goals, and with them came
gross and bitter disappointment and unhappiness . . . the loss
of her family and the destruction of her soul.

The other two had the right goals . . .
they wanted to give service and contribution
        and to have the approval of God.
They wanted to have true, strong families and the
integrity and righteousness that would give them
        self-respect.
One of the two did not know how to pursue his goals.
He knew that what he wanted was right,
and he thought about it somewhat,
and for a long time the potential for success was there.
But he did little about it, and, over the years,
his desire dimmed
and he slipped little by little to the lower, easier road
and failed at some goals and was mediocre at others.

The last person had the right goals
and the right approach.
She remained true to those goals
because she knew how to pursue them,
and her reward was joy in this world
and exaltation in the world to come.

One made it . . .
One out of four.
Each of the other three failed for a different reason:
        no goals,
        wrong goals,
        wrong method of pursuing right goals.

The setting of goals is an art.
The pursuit of goals is a skill.
And no other art, no other skill,
        can reap such fruit, such reward,
        such joy.

The goal-setting process need not start in a vacuum.
The gospel makes our lifetime goal very clear:
To return to God and to aid others in doing likewise.
That overall goal leads to some definite conclusions
regarding the general *direction* and the basic *priorities* that
our relationship goals
and our achievement goals
should take.
We know that the relationships critical to our exaltation
are with God, with self, and with family . . .
and we know that the achievements critical to our exaltation
are the working out of our own salvation
and the contributions we make to the salvation of others.

Beyond that, the goal-setting process is our own . . .
the process of turning these general directions
into *specific, reachable objectives* is ours to discover.

The discussion of relationship goals
must be separated
from the discussion of accomplishment goals
because the nature of the two is so different.
Relationships are as different from accomplishments as is
        a quiet walk in the park with a friend
                from
        the building of a giant suspension bridge.

The pursuit of relationships and the pursuit of accomplishments
are as different from each other
as is
        a rolling, lolling sea
                from
        a bolt of lightning.

The pursuit of accomplishments depends, for its success,
on planning and implementation and energy and drive.
The pursuit of relationships depends, for its success,
on sensitivity and approachability and a yielding disposition.

Accomplishment goals can be specifically set
                and specifically measured . . .
and they can be subdivided into
short-range "stepping-stone" goals that lead directly
and predictably
to longer-range goals.

Relationship goals can be set only directionally
                and measured only relatively . . .
and they are pursued by general awareness and by habits
and by the setting of priorities and programs that flow and
that improve gradually over time rather than
step by measurable step.

Achievement Goals

Achievement goals involve certain specific principles
which can be understood by
the comparison below:

The Mountain Climber	*Ourselves as Climbers Through Mortality*
In an effort to decide which peak to climb, he seeks the advice of an old and wise guide.	Without God's guidance (on our *priorities* and on our *foreordination*) we may climb the "wrong mountain."
The guide is glad to help . . . it is his work, and his satisfaction is in seeing his clients reach the summit.	God is anxious to help for *his* work is to bring about our immortality and eternal life
They counsel together taking into account the desire and ability of the man and the difficulty and requirements of the mountains . . . and a mountain is chosen.	Through prayer and spiritual effort we learn to know ourselves and strive to know God's will. With his help we *set long-range goals.*
The wise guide leaves the decision to the man, but lets the man know he's made a good decision	We are here to learn how to decide. God won't make decisions for us. But *he will tell us*

after he has.

if they are right
after we make them.

The man then determines
where he will stay
each night . . .
what plateau he will
        have reached
at the end of each day.
(The wise guide helps again.)

The only sure way
to reach
long-range goals
is to set
specific and measurable
shorter-range,
stepping-stone goals
that lead there.

Next
the path is charted
        that leads from
                plateau
                        to
        plateau
every part
of the course is
        planned carefully
and the plan is updated
        often
        as the man climbs.

After long- and short-
range goals
                are set
we must creatively
plan our time
our efforts
our actions.
We all need
regular planning sessions
in which we reassess
and correct our course.

The old guide can't go
                along

but he gives the man
a two-way radio
and asks him
to ask
for help and guidance
                often.

We solicit
God's help
through prayer . . .

and he asks us to ask . . .
(it is scripture's
most frequent
admonition).

The man puts forth	And we *work*,
all his strength	
and climbs	putting forth our
	strongest effort
the mountain.	toward the goal.

If you look at the italicized words
in the right-hand column,
a goal-setting and achieving sequence emerges.

    1. Know priorities.

    2. Seek insight and guidance regarding individual
    gifts and purpose and foreordination.

    3. Set long-range goals (based on 1 and 2).

    4. Go to the Lord for confirmation
    of the correctness of those goals.

    5. Set specific and measurable
    shorter-range, "stepping-stone goals."

    6. Hold private and regular
    planning sessions
    to simplify and review those goals
    and to plan the immediate period
            ahead.

    7. Pray.

    8. Work . . . be strong.

If it is followed properly,
this eight-step process is infallible . . .
    infallible because it engages the help
    of an infallible Being
        all along the way.

There is one caution that should be made
regarding achievement goals.
It is possible to become *too* committed to
a particular goal
and to a particular course leading to it.
Some become so obsessed with an objective
that, in effect, they put blinders on themselves
and see nothing but the goal.
> They fail to see *people.*
> They fail to see *feelings.*
> And they fail to see *better opportunities*
> > than the one they are pursuing
> > (or a better *path* to the goal they are
> > pursuing).

There is a cure for this problem . . .
an attitude that eliminates the danger of blinders
and that also
> makes goal-seeking more fun.
It is the attitude of "serendipity."

In eighteenth-century England
Horace Walpole coined a new word.
He took it from an ancient Persian fable about the
three princes of Serendip who,
while seeking their respective fortunes, found something
unexpected
which was *better* than the thing they were consciously seeking.
Walpole therefore defined *serendipity* as
"The gift, through *sagacity* and *good fortune,*
to discover something good while seeking after something else."

Most of us can identify with that word, because most of us
have had a few "serendipity" days . . .
days when good things just happen . . .
when we can seem to do no wrong . . .
when one good thing leads to another until we are

clear-headed and confident and
ready to meet the world on its own terms.

A post-Walpole group in England
(almost a sect as it turned out)
decided they could actively *seek* serendipity.
They met regularly
and determined that serendipity resulted from a state of mind.
They concluded that they could actively and productively
seek that state of mind.

I have concluded the same thing . . .
and I think there are only two requirements.

1. To be working toward definite goals with well-defined
    but flexible plans. (Walpole said that serendipity was
    discovering something good *while seeking* something else.)
    Only if you know where you want to go and have a
    route to get you there can you recognize a better
    destination or a better route when you see one.)

2. Increased awareness and appreciation . . .
    wise observation or "sagacity"
    as Walpole called it . . . so that the newer, better options
    are *seen* and *grasped* before they can go by.

Relationship Goals

Relationship goals don't work quite the same way as
achievement goals.
If you want a great relationship with your daughter,
you can't say, "By March I'll be closer to her and by
        October I'll be 60 percent close and by
        the New Year I'll be 98 percent close."
Relationship goals are not specifically graded
                or measurable or devisable . . .
so stepping-stone goals don't really work.

What does really work is an effort to *program* your mind
and your motivation toward a relationship goal . . .
to derive and plan the kind
of *activities* and *programs* and *habits*
that will lead to better relationships . . .
to develop the *approaches* and *procedures* that promote them.
And let these become good *habits*.

Family home evenings
      build family relationships.
Sincere, regular prayer
      builds a relationship with God.
Open, honest communication (and friendliness)
      builds relationships with others.

An Asian grandmother once lived next door to us
with her granddaughter.
Every evening when I came home, I saw them
together . . .
sometimes playing games,
sometimes reading stories,
sometimes blowing bubbles . . .
      always enjoying each other.
The grandmother once told me
that she thought the goal of a relationship
is met simply
by *time spent together.*

Now, the question is *how* . . .
how should relationship goals and achievement goals
be approached and pursued?

Since every person's goals are different (and they should be),
I hesitate to give an example (because it would not be
completely applicable to you).

But I will do so anyway (because the *pattern* and *sequence* and
system of the example may also work on your somewhat
different goals).

The example is a young man in graduate school
named Barney . . .
married, with two small daughters.
(Again, his goals are neither "right" nor "wrong" . . .
and are useful only as illustrations.)

Barney's basic goal diagram looks like this:

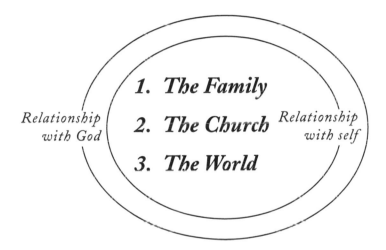

His first priority is his family,
His second priority is his church,
and all his priories are surrounded and
influenced by his relationships
with himself and with God.

Each of the three priorities involve and are dependent on
    relationships . . .
so he fills in his diagram to include
the habits he hopes will mold each relationship.

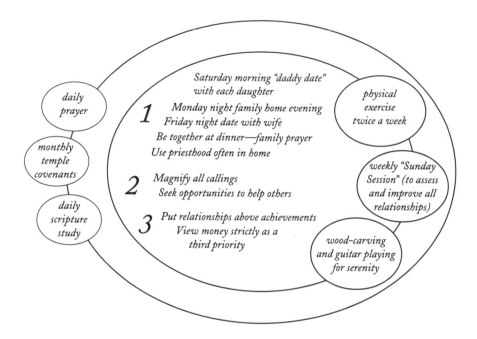

You can see that Barney's relationship goals consist mostly of habits
and programs
and attitudes that he is trying to develop . . .
practices that he feels will improve and strengthen his relationships.

The diagram for his relationship goals
pretty much stays the same, year after year
(except Barney perfects it as he comes up with
better programs and ideas).

Another way (perhaps the most specific way)
to set relationship goals
is by writing in a private place, perhaps your journal,
a projected *description* of a particular relationship
as you want it to be in three years.

Describe your relationship with your spouse
(or your child, or parent, or sibling, or friend)
as you'd like it to be.
Project yourself out three years and write in the present tense.
Don't say, "I'm not a writer."
Just write.
No one will read this but you.
Don't say, "But I'll be too idealistic and I'll never measure up."
Remember the ideal!
After all, a goal is a target.
Aim for the bull's eye and with the bull's eye in mind
you'll get closer and closer!

Write a short projected description for
each important relationship.
Read them (and add to them) every month or so.
Let their idealism, like a magnet,
pull on and draw in and transform your reality.

Pursuit by Attitude

We stretched out on a Puerto Rico beach one day . . .
relaxed . . . my Linda and I.
It was the end of the working part of a three-day trip,
and things had gone well.
We had achieved the objectives
for which we had come and the accomplishments made us feel
worthwhile,
and the worthwhile feeling took our minds off of ourselves
and let us talk openly and easily.

We talked for hours in the sun that day
about almost everything.

As the relationship brought us closer,
and as we basked in a recent achievement as well
                    as in the sun,
the joy level welled up from inside,
and through the vehicle of our bodies and our minds
                    the prompters of joy gave us Joy 2.

Total, open relationships tend to progress to
higher levels of conversation.
First we talked of things . . . the sea, the sky, the city,
the weather.
Then we talked of people . . . our children (at home with
grandma),
the friends we would see that night, the new
people we'd meet.
Finally we talked about concepts and ideas . . .
and one of the things that occurred to us
was the notion of *waves* and *lightning,*
and our conclusion that these two symbols
could represent the two attitudes
that contribute most to
relationships and to achievements
and thus produce the most Joy 2.

The thought unfolded in this sequence:

1.   Accomplishments are one of the things that make us happy.

2.   Relationships are the other.

3.   Everything that prompts happiness fits into one of these
       two categories.

4.   There is a particular mood . . . a certain frame of mind
      that leads to each of the two.

5.   Achievements generally happen when we are
      active, animated, filled with élan.

6.   Relationships happen best in moods of calm,
      secure, relaxed, reflective quietude.

7.   Since there is no accurate single word to describe
      either of the two moods or frames of mind, we'll *coin*
      some. The achievement-producing mood is akin to
      "lightning" . . . things happen sharply and crisply,
      like a series of connecting check marks, one
      leading to another. The relationship-producing mood is
      akin to "waves" . . . an easy flow of peaks and valleys . . .
      unhurried, unforced.

8.   The symbols describe the moods better than words do.

9.   These are the only truly productive moods,
      because achievements and relationships are the
      two categories of things that have real value.

10.   One leads to the other and vice versa.
           ⁄⁄⁄ produces the security and ego-satisfaction
      that permits enough relaxation and freedom of thought
      to get to ∿∿. And ∿∿ in turn, through
      its relationships (with self as well as others), produces
      the ideas and goals for the next ⁄⁄⁄ mood to
      implement and achieve.

11. Most people spend a very small percentage of
     their time in either of the two productive moods.

12. While we are seldom *in* either of the productive moods,
     we are almost always close to one or the other.
     A hyperactive frustration may need only a certain
     channeling and direction to become ⚡.
     A tired, pensive, and mellow mood may be only steps
     away from
     constructive, reflective 〰.

13. It is possible, through awareness and understanding of
     the two productive
     moods, to nudge yourself from 〰's negative
     counterpart (depression, sullenness) into the positive
     relationship of 〰; and to nudge yourself
     from ⚡'s negative counterpart (nervousness, agitation)
     into the positive *achievement* of ⚡.

There are a few particular concepts
that I think "flesh in" the philosophy
of waves and lightning.
Each concept can be represented by a *single word* or a word pair.

These are twenty favorite words of mine . . .
words that describe the various facets
          of waves and lightning . . .
words that, when taken together, describe
          the type of person I would like to be . . .
words that I believe, through awareness and thought,
          can program a person's mind and attitude
          and greatly aid in the pursuit of Joy 2.

Some words (concepts)
apply primarily to 〰
(and thus lead to better relationships).
Others apply mainly to ⚡ (and to achievement).

I have arranged the words so that the first ones
        apply primarily to ⌇⌇⌇⌇
        and the last ones
        primarily to ⟋ .
        (The middle ones apply to both.)

Keep in mind that the descriptions and definitions
I am giving to the words
go well beyond their traditional, dictionary definitions.
Each is a *concept* that I think can be *represented*
by a single word:

1. *Ask*
A three-letter word that constitutes
the most repeated admonition in scripture . . .
a key that unlocks the blessings of heaven
from a God so committed
to our agency
that he withholds his initiative until we extend ours
by asking.
Good asking prompts good listening
in prayer
and in conversation.
"Ask and listen" is a three-word key
to good relationships in every setting
and can unlock the solution
that we call communication.

2. *Peaceable*
Soft and easy, so calm
that you can slow time down.
It's Satan that the scriptures describe as
"*rushing*" to and fro in the earth.
On the flip side, scripture speaks of
"the peaceable things . . . that which bringeth joy."
To be easy to be around, to be easily entreated,
to move and think with the slow, gentle grace of faith.

93

Jesus always had time
for people, for beauty, for the joy or needs
of the present moment.
To be peaceable is to have a deep inner core
unaffected by surface storms,
to feel the Spirit,
to be still and know.

3. *Consultant*
A manipulator, a dictator, even a manager
seeks to impose his will on others
to control them.
More welcomed, more appreciated, more often befriended
(and more effective over the long run)
is a *consultant*.
The difference is that a consultant helps us with
our goals, *our* agenda.
The others use us within
their goals, their agenda.
I'd rather have others, from my children
to my friends,
see me as one interested in them,
as one interested in their interests, their success,
their joy.

4. *Soft Sell*
I remember once, when we were in the market
for a new home,
many realtors gave us strong, overbearing *pitches*
on various houses . . . on their great virtues
and our great need for them.

One realtor (an older, Russian-born immigrant)
came over and *listened* . . .
found out exactly what we wanted . . .
asked questions . . .
got to know us . . . seemed to enjoy the whole thing.

He sold us a house
>   (and we later learned that, in his slow, soft way,
>   he sold more homes
>   than anyone else in the area).

The world often associates success with "the hard sell" . . .
with a relentless, insensitive drive.

In fact, any success achieved with this pattern
is hollow and empty.
True success comes through the soft sell . . .
>   through calmness and serenity . . .
>   through more thought and less flashing action . . .
>   through putting relationships ahead of achievements . . .
>   through taking time for beauty, for people, for
>   observation.

5. *Windows*
A selfish person looks into mirrors and sees every situation
in terms of how it will affect him.
A more selfless, more Christlike person looks through windows
and sees how others are affected, how others feel.

It is eternally interesting
that the way to *seek* joy is to give joy.

If only we could learn that lesson . . .
it would not only bring us joy . . .
it would improve our performance in every aspect
of life.
If we would try a little less to make our neighbors *good*
and try a little harder to make our neighbors *happy* . . .
then we would be happier,
they would be happier,
we would be less self-righteous,
and they would have a better chance of ultimately becoming
good because of our actions.

Certain definite rules apply to "windows."
1. Smile.
2. Remember names and faces and details.
3. Never argue or tell people they are wrong.
4. Listen.
5. Talk about the other person's interests.
6. Praise and compliment.
7. Ask, "How do you *feel* about . . . ?"
8. Be considerate in small things.
9. Be honest and open.

Now, at first glance you may say that this list reads like
                    Dale Carnegie or Og Mandino . . .
but at second glance you'll see that it also reads like
                    the gospel.

6. *Child*
"Self help" (ultimately an oxymoron, by the way)
tells us to actualize by self-confidence.
"I can do anything!"
The gospel tells us to reach by humble faith.
"I can do nothing,
but God working through me can do all."
"Child" is what we literally are to God
and what we must think ourselves to draw his power.
Remembering his greatness and our nothingness,
said King Benjamin,
assures us of continual forgiveness
and continual rejoicing.

7. *Graphic*
Graphic is the poetic and
                    artistic
          way of viewing life . . .

it is seeing as the poet sees . . .
　　　　sees things for their beauty,
　　　　　　　　their design,
　　　　　　　　their uniqueness.

I have a poetic aunt who looks at an ordinary tree
and sees unique patterns in the bark . . .
one-of-a-kind designs in the limbs . . .
symbols of people in the shaped configuration of the leaves.
She looks at a city street (which others see as dirty and ugly)
and sees radiance and relationships,
tradition and texture.

There is a graphic way of dressing,
　　　　a graphic way of looking at a sunset,
　　　　a graphic way of giving a speech,
　　　　a graphic way of writing a letter,
　　　　a graphic way of planning a date,
　　　　　　　a presentation, a family home evening,
　　　　　　　a day, a life.

Graphic is going and saying things in a unique, crisp,
style-marked way . . .
It is classic simplification.
It is one precise word instead of a paragraph,
and one picture instead of a thousand words.

Graphic is to have flair . . . to have pizzazz . . .
to avoid the common way or method just
for the sake of being unique.

Graphic is grace and relaxed sureness . . .
the ability to conceptualize
and to draw pure, hard, clear decisions.

8. *Synergy*
While the world seeks independence,
the Spirit prompts dependence on God
and interdependence with family and friends.
The best interdependence
is synergy
where love, mutual confidence, and complementing qualities
make the total greater
than the sum of its parts.
Marriage is the highest opportunity for synergy,
but it can come in every relationship
where we love and give.

9. *Touch*
That extra touch that transfers good to best,
the touch that tells intimacy,
the deft touch of subtle rotation on a free throw,
or a drop volley.
Touch is the conscious application
of feeling,
the touch of the Master's hand.
Those whose lives we touch
who?
and how?

10. *Ambassador*
"Take upon them the name of thy Son" (D&C 20:77).
Thus, his representatives. His stewards.
More than an instrument in his hands . . .
Ambassadors in his service.
What other self-image could more encourage us
to avoid dark and seek light,
to climb over fear and doubt,
and be the best we can be
for him.

11. *Stewardship*

An ownership mentality
produces envy and jealousy toward those with more,
and pride and condescension to those below.
It aims disproportionate energy at pseudo "achievement"
and makes some relationships feel like slavery.
It is also a basic error, since God owns all.
Its opposite truth, *stewardship*,
exchanges peace for stress
and grows tolerance, empathy,
and perhaps the meekness
that will inherit the earth.

12. *Lateral Thinking*

A young girl faced a dilemma:
the creditor was going to jail her father
unless she married him.
She pleaded for mercy.
The villain deceptively said he'd give her one
chance . . . that he'd put a black marble
and a white one in a hat . . . and that if she
could pull out the white, he would
release her father from debt and leave them
both alone.
He then secretly put two black marbles in the hat.
The girl drew a marble (concealed in her hand),
then quickly let it slip,
unseen,
down the heating vent.
She then made an apology for dropping it
and proceeded to explain that, since a black
marble remained in the hat,
the one she had drawn was obviously white.
She was saved by lateral thinking.

Lateral thinking is creative thinking.
It is turning adversity into success.
It is making common things uncommon.
It is working by faith and by thought
rather than by physical force.
It is a halfback bouncing along the defensive line
running laterally, looking for daylight . . .
rather than a fullback, lowering his head and plowing
right into the opposition . . .
It is walking around to the
back door
instead of trying to knock down
the locked front door.

13. *Fertile Soil*
We had a fellow named Joe on our tennis team.
His greatest problem was lack of confidence.
His strokes were good,
but he talked to himself.
It was tough to play next to him because
he was always saying,
"Oh, no, Joe, what a bad shot!"
or sarcastically,
"Oh, yes, Joe, wasn't that just dandy! Right in the net."
He never seemed to enjoy the game.
Even when he won he commented on how poorly he'd
played and how his mistakes had almost lost it.
We got a new coach the next year
who taught Joe a lesson about tennis
and me a lesson about life.
He said:
> "Your own self-criticism damages your confidence
> even more than the criticism from others . . .
> Your mind is like *fertile soil* . . . It
> will return what you plant.
> Tell yourself you're lousy and you will be.
> Tell yourself you're great and you will be."

Too many of us avoid complimenting ourselves
because we
mistake confidence for conceit and confuse
love of self with self-centeredness.
We assume that people who are confident and
like themselves are not able to be as sensitive
to others.
The opposite is true . . . confidence and
self-love allow people to
quit worrying about themselves and their abilities . . .
in short, to be less wrapped up in themselves
and therefore to have more time and concern for others.

14. *Serendipity*
While I'm thinking about that tennis coach,
I remember that he also believed
that people play their best tennis when they are relaxed . . .
that being too tense,
       too forced,
       too controlled,
       too worried,
       can ruin anyone's game.
He used to tell us to forget about the score and
to think about the beauty of the game
             and of the day . . .
to appreciate the body and the racket . . .
          to love the ball and concentrate on it.
He said that the good, pure, natural stroke
was in all of us and we should
just relax
and be positive and let it come out.

Life is so much like tennis.
The worried, forced, nervous person
tries too hard, makes mistakes he shouldn't make,
         and misses obvious opportunities.

Serendipity is the ability to be relaxed and calm
at the same time as being sensitive and sagacious . . .
thus becoming "able to find good things
while seeking something else."

There is more on serendipity earlier in this chapter.
It is the beautiful quality
of being able to find good in all things,
of being the calm master of all situations,
and of being able to see new approaches and
new openings leading to both old
and new objectives.

15. *Order*
Chaos breeds confusion and doubt,
        but order breeds confidence and clarity.

Disorganized effort is ineffective and wasted,
        but three feet of focused sunlight can cut through steel.

There are three main kinds of order,
                and one leads to the next.

        1. *Thing* order. A material and physical
        "in-place-ness" creates a pleasing environment,
        allows us to find things; and, somehow,
        external organization leads to internal organization.

        2. *Thought* order. Clear objectives and
        plans allow us to categorize thoughts and
        benefit from them as they come.

        3. *Role* order. When objectives and knowledge
        are in order, we can best judge our own
        role
        in the scheme of things.
        The head-of-the-family father's role

and the heart-of-the-family mother's role
will then be self-evident rather than arbitrary.

16. *Pizazz*
Words like *mundane* or *average*
or *rut*
need an antonym, an antithesis, an antidote.
It is *pizazz,*
breaking out,
giving something an extra flare,
some unique style.
Pizazz is like a spice:
it can be stirred into a date, a party,
a family home evening,
a presentation, a term paper, even a
simple Saturday afternoon.
It can make boring tasks fun,
and it can put a smile on faces
that have been without for too long.

17. *Light*
The light of Christ,
elder brother to all lesser relatives of light.
All—even small— standing forth against
darkness and its prince.
The light of truth, the recognized ring of it
prompting both faith and discernment.
Light lifts, light creates,
light casts out fear,
light brings things to pass.

18. *Best*
Strange as it sounds,
it is often easier to be *best* than to be *good.*
Most men strive to do well
        but the notion of being *best* occurs to very few.

The ranks of those whose goal it is to be good
are crowded,
and competition is fierce because all are
working toward common, traditional goals
set by who-knows-who but pursued by almost all.
The ranks of those who wish to go *above* that norm . . .
to be best . . . are thin.
(The west face of Everest is never crowded.)

One who sets his sights a bit higher . . .
who follows his own drummer . . .
who looks always for a better, more unique way . . .
this man will be not good, but best.
He will learn to work by faith
      (by mental and spiritual effort and not by blind physical
force).
He will learn to achieve in beautifully conceived
                    brilliant bursts.
And he will learn that
good is the enemy of best.

19. *Midas*
Money can be the facilitator or enabler of a worthy cause
(or the by-product of one) . . .
it should never be thought of as more.

Money can bring freedom
      (and allow the pursuit of more worthy goals)
or it can bring enslavement
      (and curtail the pursuit of anything else).

Turn over financial management to the Lord
by telling him that money is *not* your goal . . .
that it is *not* your priority . . .
that you intend to work hard but that you view money as a
by-product and that
if you need it for your foreordination
        you trust that he will see that you have it
and if you don't
        he won't.

I think a good, simple, workable rule is to
take out a fixed percentage of your increase
for yourself (for saving)
at exactly the same moment you take out
ten percent for the Lord.
If you do that consistently and without exception,
it can hardly help but give you an eventual degree
of financial freedom.

20. *Elan*
I go to a barber
whom I saw undergo a change for the worse.
For months I had been amazed at his
buoyancy and happiness.
He came from Brazil, and
every time I went in we talked about
his dream of returning, or taking his
family and going back.
He had great plans and ideas . . . he glowed as he
talked of them.
        But the time came when
        he lost his dream; he said he had decided
        it would never work, that he wouldn't be able
        to find a job . . . that inflation would eat up his savings.
        He was a sad man now . . .

he seemed somehow smaller
and darker
and less alive,
and my haircut was the worst he'd ever given me . . .
He had lost his dream.

Elan is a craving for action.
Elan is having a dream and working toward it.
Elan is to be totally enthralled with
something.
Elan brings a magic and a magnetism . . .
it lends light to the soul and
demands action and experience rather than
security and protection.
      Elan is the enthusiasm that turns
      mud puddles into geysers
      and ordinary people into great leaders.

Modify these word/concepts, or substitute
your own adjectives until they become a description of
who you want to be.
Then try self-programming them into your subconscious so they
become
more prominently involved in who you are.
I do this as I run
(why not tune the mind along with
the muscles and the cardiovascular).
I go through the words, convincing myself
that each one describes me.
"I am graphic and poetic—just yesterday I found a
dramatic three-dimensional demonstration
to make my point in the meeting."
"I am serendipity this morning. I delayed
a conference call so I could talk
to George who called unexpectedly
from London. He gave me a very
promising idea that I'm going

to use in next month's meeting."
Then on to the next word . . .
It even makes the jogging less boring.

Pursuit of Joy 2—Overview

Joy 2 is pursued by pursuing achievements and relationships.
  Achievements are pursued by
  specific, stepping-stone *objectives*
  and by creative, positive *attitudes.*
      Relationships are pursued by
      priorities, programs, and
      projected relationship descriptions . . .
      and by yielding, sharing, other-centered
      attitudes and habits.

One great beauty of relationships and achievements
(and one good reason not to be discouraged
when either is tough to reach)
is that there is great inherent joy
in their *pursuit*
as well as in their accomplishment.

Throughout these pages it has been noted that
relationships and achievements lead inescapably
to the feeling of Joy 2.
What has not been noted until right now
(but what is equally true)
is that the feeling of Joy 2 brings a confidence that
leads directly and surely
to *more* achievement . . . to *higher* achievement . . .
and to *more* relationships . . . to *deeper* relationships.

Thus the spiral diagram works again.

*More relationships
and achievements*

More Joy 2

7

The Expander of Joy
Knowledge and Truth

1. The Vehicle of Joy
Our second estate—
earth, bodies, agency
(physical)

2. The Enhancers or Prompters
Relationships and
accomplishments
(social/emotional)

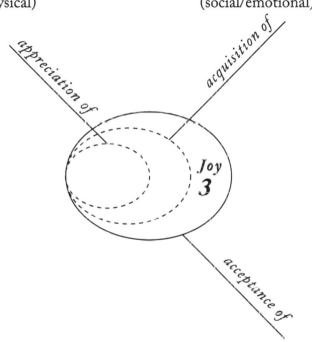

3. The Expander of Joy
Knowledge, truth,
and testimony
(mental/spiritual)

Six Stories: Part Three

Put your fingers in the book at page 21 and at page 58
so that you can flip back to parts one and two
of each story before you read part three.

"The Flower and the Camera"—Part Three

One day you learn about flowers,
about roots, chlorophyll, and photosynthesis,
about this perennial and how it reblooms each year.
Another day you learn about cameras:
shutter speed, f-stops, focal length, and exposure,
how your print is the plant's express image.
Your joy is expanded
by knowledge.
(to be continued)

"The First Lawn Mowing"—Part Three

Last week Dad explained how grass grows . . .
showed the seeds and also
explained why mowing it helps it grow.
The understanding adds the dimensions of insight and *purpose*
to what they feel, and takes their joy to the third level.
(to be continued)

"The Love Story"—Part Three

John and Mary each had some degree
of individual faith and testimony
which combined to form a collective spiritual insight that was
more than double what either had possessed before.
This spiritual synergy
awakened new thoughts, new spirituality; and
they pondered together
the beauty of the preexistence
(in which they felt they knew each other)

and the hereafter (in which, they believed,
they and their children
could always be together in the presence of God).
(to be continued)

"The Marriage"—Part Three
The thought occurs now, to both,
of looking into each other's eyes again later, in eternity.
There is joy in
knowing what the relationship has become in the two years
since they met, and in
anticipating what it will become in two million years.
And there is also Joy 3
in thinking backward and wondering if their spiritual hands
touched there also.
And as great as are the anticipated and reflected joys,
the greatest joy is in the knowledge of the present . . .
the knowledge that this joy
is the purpose of life . . . that it is what God
wants us to feel while we are here . . .
that the procreation resulting from this union
and the developing oneness of the relationship
is pleasing to God, is the object of this earth and this life,
and is, in fact,
the very element of which Godhood is made.
(to be continued)

"The New Arrival"—Part Three

You turn your thoughts from the earthly reference
to the eternal and look down again
at the nestled infant on your arm . . .
thinking of him this time not as a baby but as a brother
who shared a preexistence with you . . .
who likely was one of the choice spirits reserved to come
in these critical latter days.

He is God's child, and God, in supreme love,
has given you the godlike experience of
physical parenthood . . . of stewardship
over one of his choice sons.
Your mind shifts again, from backward to forward . . .
to the celestial kingdom
where you can continue to be with husband and family and
with this newcomer for eternity . . .
progressing together in ways you haven't even dreamed of yet.
This knowledge expands your feeling to Joy 3.
(to be continued)

"The Promotion"—Part Three

Reflection, later that night:
Perks and power and people's recognition are great,
but where do they fit in the eternal scheme?
Can I do this without negative impact on my family,
on my church assignments?
I feel it has come through faith and prayer,
so I believe I can *balance* it
by those same means.
(to be continued)

Glimpses of the Joy of Knowledge and Truth

Joseph Smith said that
joy comes through a knowledge of God;[1]
and in each of the six stories, as in life itself,
it is easy to see
how gospel truth and insight
expand and extend Joy 1 and Joy 2 into Joy 3.

---

1. *Teachings of the Prophet Joseph Smith*, p. 57.

There is Joy 1 in a sunset,
> but there is Joy 3 in understanding that
> that sun
> was made for us by a loving Father.

There is Joy 1 in a strong, healthy body
> but there is Joy 3 in understanding that
> that body
> is in the image and likeness of God's body
> (and that it can ultimately be perfected
> as his is).

There is Joy 2 in a beautiful friendship,
> but there is Joy 3 in understanding that
> that friendship
> may have started before this mortal earth was made
> and may continue to exist after it.

There is Joy 2 in attaining a graduate degree,
> but there is Joy 3 in understanding that
> the learning and experience it represents
> are some of the purposes for which we came to earth
> and can be taken with us when we leave.

There is a close connection
between joy and understanding.
Almost everything that is enjoyable
is *more* enjoyable if it is understood.

I remember once when I saw a beautiful
underwater film of a large trout
taking the bait, being caught, then released.
I noticed things about his sense of smell,
about his beautiful movements in the water,
about his magnificent struggle, his speed and freedom in release.
I had always loved to go fishing, but the next time I went

I liked it even more
because I understood what was happening down there.

One Saturday night
I told my little girl a bedtime story.
Her eyes lit up at the exciting parts
and her little brow furrowed when it looked as if
the heroine was in distress.
Her whole face broke into delight
when the hero saved the day and all lived
happily ever after.
The next morning, in the
Sunday School class I went to,
the lesson was on the eternal nature of families . . .
backward to the preexistence,
forward to the celestial kingdom.
I thought all that day about
what a short time it had been since my little girl
had departed the Father's presence
and entrusted herself
to me.
And I thought (with such emotion
that my heart pounded)
about the joy of being with her always.

That night I told her another
story,
and this time I saw even beyond
the light and love . . .
I saw *through* her eyes and *beyond* her face
and loved her soul with mine.

I *enjoyed* my relationship with my little girl on Saturday night,
but I *loved* the one on Sunday even more
because I was more aware and understood more
about the length and breadth and eternal bonds
of that relationship.

Imagine two men
watching a basketball game.
        One man understands the game . . .
        knows its objectives, its techniques,
        knows the rules and how the score is kept,
        and has a strong partisan favoritism
        for one of the two teams.
            The other man is unfamiliar with the game . . .
            has no knowledge of its goals, its participants.

To the first man the game is thrilling and exciting,
                                    agonizing and exhilarating.

He becomes a participant in it
by virtue of his cheers and reaction.

        To the second man the game is
        at times boring,
        at times paradoxical,
        and at times perplexing.

It is understanding that makes the difference . . .
both in the basketball game
and in life.

Like putting something under convex glass . . .
understanding enlarges joy.

Truth makes us free . . .
the glory of God is intelligence . . .
knowledge is power . . .
understanding is joy . . .

Truth and spiritual knowledge are the
expanders of joy
because they *interpret* Joy 1 and Joy 2 and
allow us to understand

and fully appreciate our bodies,
our earth, our agency, our relationships, our achievements . . .
and to comprehend both their purpose and their beauty.

Understanding and comprehension build joy.
Confusion and ignorance and lack of understanding build fear.

Light expands and intensifies when
a person seeks and finds and studies and understands
truth.
Whether in a book, through a conversation,
by direct observation . . .

>whatever its source,
>truth is light,
>and light is joy.

Through Joseph Smith, God said that intelligence is His glory
(D&C 93:36),
and told us to seek it through *all* sources (D&C 88:78–80).
This he said
because he knows that
truth is the key to the goal of joy.

There is joy in *gaining* truth.
There is joy in *applying* that truth, personally, to our lives.

Knowledge of our origin, our purpose, and our destination
makes it easier
to appreciate
the past,
the present,
and the future portions of our mortal lives . . .
(and easier to derive joy from each . . .
from past memories,
from present experience,
from future expectations).

It allows us to see the joy in each stage of life.
The joy (and innocence and freedom from care) of childhood.
The joy (and frustration and transition) of adolescence.
The joy (and responsibility) of early marriage and family.
The joy (and other-helping potential) of middle age.
The joy (and posterity and influence) of older age.
Each phase is beautiful
      and wonderful . . .
Each should be, in its own time,
      the current "best part of life."

Joy, in this context, is not something you find
but something you *keep* finding and refinding
over and over
in different forms
and in different places.
It is gospel insight and knowledge that allows this.

Truth Leads to Freedom and Confidence

It is the knowledge that God loves us
      that allows us to more fully love ourselves
      and that gives us the Joy 3 that comes from being
      loved.

It is the knowledge of the preexistence and of God's plan
      that lets us know that we have the same personalities
      and the same characteristics now that we had then;
      that tells us this earth is the time and place to
      purge and purify them,
      and that gives us the Joy 3 that comes as we improve.

It is the gospel's insight that makes more simple
        the much-discussed goal of
        "finding self"
        and that gives us Joy 3 in the ultimate security
            of knowing who we are.

It is the knowledge of our relationship to God
        that gives us the confidence of knowing that
        we are his children and have access to his help . . .
        and the humility of knowing that he owns all
        and that
        we are mere stewards.
        (This gives us the otherwise impossible
        Joy 3 combination of
        confident humility.)

It is the knowledge of life's purpose
        that allows us to order our lives,
        to weed out the superfluities,
        and that gives us the Joy 3 of correct priorities
        properly sought and actually found.

It is gospel perspective that allows us
        to see things in an eternal scope,
        to make decisions on the basis of eternal implications,
        to have the joy of planning eternity,
        and the joy of knowing that the good things we gain
        (our learning and our relationships)
        can be ours forever.

Any truth from any source increases freedom,
and true freedom yields true joy.
Think of a baby girl.
She learns to walk and is free from confinement and immobility.
She learns to talk and is free from social confinement and isolation.
She learns to read and is free from ignorance and illiteracy.
She learns to write and is free to preserve her thoughts.
She learns to love and is free to be Christlike.

Now think of humankind.
We discover fire and are free from cold.
We discover speech and are free from mental isolation.
We discover the wheel and are free from heavy burdens.
We discover the domestication of horses and are free
        from the slowness and restricted range of walking.
We discover astronomy and are free from fear and superstition.
We discover cultivation and food preservation and are free
        from hunger and forced migration.
We discover writing and are free
        from forgetting what we want to remember.
We discover ships and sails and are free
        from geographic restriction.
We discover vaccines and serums and are free
        from disease.

Thus the joy of truth is both direct and indirect . . .
direct because the discovery of truth
                contains inherent joy,
indirect because truth brings freedom,
                and freedom brings joy.

There is an interesting "chain reaction equation"
which some have discovered consciously . . .
others subconsciously.

It is: That intense interest always leads to learning . . .
and learning usually leads to understanding . . .
and understanding always leads to confidence.

There is also a counter-equation:
Lack of interest leads to wasted, non-learning time . . .
which results in misunderstanding or no understanding . . .
which, in turn, prompts fear.

Thus, if you seek confidence,
cultivate interest.

      Did you notice above that the one place where
      "usually"
      replaced "always"
      (the one weak link in the equation)
      is the learning-to-understanding step.
      Not all people properly understand
      what they learn . . . some are "ever learning,
      and never able to come to the knowledge
      of the truth" (2 Timothy 3:7).

      Here, then, is why our learning must
      be guided by the Spirit . . .
      so that we will understand what we learn . . .
      so that we will know the "whys"
      as well as the "whats."

Answers of the Restored Church

I once asked a group of young people to list
the ten questions
they felt were most relevant . . . the ten to which
known answers
would have the greatest inherent value . . .
the ten most important questions
                    for mankind.

The purpose of the exercise was to see
how many of their questions
could be answered by the gospel.
More specifically, I wanted to see how many
                   of the questions
were *answerable* by the complete, restored Church of
Jesus Christ,
and *non-answerable* by the rest of Christianity.

The result was astounding.

The restored Church of Jesus Christ was the only Christian
church with a solid answer for *any* of them
(and it answered them all).

Let me list those ten questions,
along with two sets of answers . . .
one, the turned-around, sometimes distorted and
sometimes counterproductive answers
        of most traditional Christianity
                        (in the left-hand column);

two, the true, restored, useful, and joyful answers of the gospel
                        (in the right-hand column).

1. *What is the nature of God?*

God is a formless spirit
everywhere but nowhere.
He is a trinity—three Gods,
but really only one;
one God, but really three.

God the Father is a perfected
man with a perfected physical
body. His son Jesus Christ also
has a body and is the Creator
and God of this world as well
as our Savior. The third
member of the Godhead is
the Holy Ghost, who is a spirit
in the shape of a man, and
whose mission is to reveal truth.

2. *What is the nature of man?*

Mankind is inherently evil
and is an enemy to God.

Mankind is God's spiritual
offspring, and we are potential
gods.

3. *What is man's relationship to God?*

God created us.
(That is about all we know.)

God is our Father, the literal
Father of our spirits. He sent us
here so that we could learn

and progress and thus become more like him.

4. *How does God communicate with man?*

He doesn't anymore— at least, not directly. He gave us the Bible; that is his word and it is all we need.

He guides his Church in three ways:
1. Through direct revelation to his chosen prophets.
2. Through the organization of his Church.
3. Through four books of sacred scripture.
In addition, all of God's children may receive revelation to guide their own lives.

5. *Where did we come from . . . what is our origin?*

No previous existence. We started when we were born on earth.

From a preexistence where we lived with our Heavenly Father and *elected* to come to this earth to prove ourselves and to gain experience and growth.

6. *Why are we here on earth . . . for what purpose?*

There are mixed opinions. As a curse, perhaps (the curse of these frail, sickly bodies), or possibly because God wanted to start us in a place that would make us appreciate heaven.

To gain the great learning and experience and capacities that are available only through a physical earth and a mortal body (a body which makes us more like God), and as a test of our worthiness to live with him eternally.

7. *Where are we going when we die?*

To heaven or to hell. Heaven is a place of eternal relaxation and rest. Hell is an eternal torment—physical, mental, or both. (Some say eternal fire.)

After resurrection, to the degree of glory we have *merited.* If we are righteous, to the celestial kingdom where God dwells, a place of accelerated eternal progression. In a lower kingdom, people are damned in the sense that water is—their progress is restricted.

8. *What about those who don't hear of Christ during their lifetime?*

They are damned. We are powerless to help the dead. (Some do say that prayers for the dead may help.)

They have an equal chance (in the spirit world) after death to accept or reject the gospel. Salvation is then possible through vicarious ordinances done on earth.

9. *Where does man get the authority to act for God?*

Through a feeling of being called, plus a diploma earned from an accredited divinity school.

By the laying on of hands by those holding the priesthood. Authority can be traced by current priesthood holders (in six or seven steps) directly back to Jesus Christ, who restored it to the earth through Peter, James, and John.

10. *What is necessary for salvation?*

Divided views. Some see church membership and its sacraments as necessary and believe those not baptized will suffer for Adam's original sin.

Christ overcame both physical and spiritual death, countering Adam's "transgression," which caused the first, and paying for our sins to overcome the second.

For others, faith in Christ is
the only requirement and
works and actions are
irrelevant.

Our sins are removed (and
we are saved) only through
our righteousness—through
both faith and works, including
the necessary ordinances.

The Single Source of Truth

When a man plants a lawn,
waters it,
weeds it,
feeds it,
mows it,
it is easy for him to begin to think
he *made* the lawn . . .
and that wrong assumption does not make him
enjoy the lawn more—rather, it makes him enjoy it
less than he would if
his attitude were one of stewardship, of humility,
and of wonder at the ability of each of
those million tiny shoots
to turn green and grow.

When a man gains new knowledge,
studies,
works,
thinks,
concludes,
it is easy for him to begin to think that
he created or at least independently discovered the truth . . .
and that wrong assumption makes the truth
less valuable and less useful
than if his attitude were one of stewardship
and if he realized
that the truth was given to him by
the Holy Ghost.

In the Church, we are taught that
by the power of the Holy Ghost
we may know the truth of all things (Moroni 10:5).
The concept of an "infinite intelligence,"
        or a "galactic source of knowledge,"
        or some sort of super-terrestrial guidance
that produces "flashes of insight"
in a thinking man's mind
        and takes him to conclusions which
                he has not arrived at through
                        any logical thought process
                        or analysis
. . . such a concept is not uncommon
                        among scientists
                        and philosophers
                        and others who probe and search
                        for new knowledge.

Many will admit
that their greatest ideas, their most important discoveries,
came in a sudden and unexpected
burst of thought
and led them in directions
                not contemplated previously.

In my small way I
have experienced these "flashes of insight"
                (but I know their real name to be
                "inspiration from the Holy Ghost").
I know there are some concepts in this book
that I hadn't learned previously,
that I hadn't read before,
and that did not evolve
as logical conclusions from any analysis I had done.

They came into my mind somewhat like
a passing glance through a keyhole
into a room I had seen before
but long since forgotten . . .
and I am surer of *their* truth
than of the truth of anything else herein.

One man said that
"the only thing more exciting than learning
is creating."
An interesting variation on that theme is
that creating *is* learning
(in its most pure and advanced and remarkable form).
Creating is the "flash-of-insight" kind of learning . . .
it is the kind where the teacher is the Holy Ghost.

8

The Pursuit of Joy 3

So many miss out on Joy 3
for the simple lack of desire to pursue it.
So many say they know the gospel is true, but
so few can say they really know the gospel.

We may think we've learned it in Sunday School classes
or in the hundreds of sermons we've heard preached
(or from the classes *we've* taught or the sermons *we've* preached).

But the gospel is not some simple set of elements that is
either known or not known—like multiplication tables
or the spelling of a word.
It is known by degree, and
there is no ceiling or limit to that knowledge.

Prophets tell us that in their lifetimes of study they have barely
scratched the surface.
And they tell us that if we will study and pray,
if we will hunger and thirst after truth,
it will distill upon our souls as the dew from heaven
and fill our hearts with joy.
　　　　This is Joy 3 . . . the joy of comprehending
　　　　and understanding the purposes and the reasons.

Joy 3 is the joy of light and the joy of freedom.
Light and truth make us free.
Freedom from ignorance opens us to higher joy.
Truth is learned in many ways . . .
Let's examine some of them now.

Learning by Study

I remember once asking a wise and knowledgeable man
to tell me a good system
for studying the scriptures.
I've never forgotten his answer.
He said:
>   "I can give you a system for eating,
>   but it's best to just be hungry."

It is the desire and not the system
that is important.
There is some reason to believe, however,
that the disciplined implementation
of a scripture-reading system
may *awaken* the desire,
which will then feed on itself until it becomes strong
and enduring.

So if you design a system,
view it partly as a means to help you awaken the desire.

I know of five somewhat unique systems (each suggested
by a different friend).
One of them might jog your mind
toward something workable for you.

1. *The Transition System*

There are two transitions every twenty-four hours:
day to night and night to day,
awake to asleep and asleep to awake.
>   Friend "A" read at least a verse or two at each.
>   He said that scripture at the morning transition
>   prepared him mentally to be a Christian all day
>   (even when driving to work on a crowded freeway).
>   He said that scripture at the evening transition
>   relaxed his soul
>   so that he slept better and awoke stronger.

He also said that he thought the two transition periods
were the best and most beautiful parts of the day, but
were wasted by most people.
Sleeping too late wastes the morning one,
watching television too late wastes the evening one,
reading a scripture makes them both
more beautiful.

> He said he didn't always read a *lot*,
> but he always read something.

2. *The Outline System*
Friend "B" said he thought mere reading was a rather
ineffective way of learning.
He said people learn more when they teach than
when they're taught,
and more when they write than when they read.
So he made outlines of the scriptures:

> a chronological outline of Christ's life . . .

> a topical outline of the Doctrine and Covenants . . .

> a geographical outline of early Book of Mormon migra-
tions . . .

> and so on.

He learned more in the active creation of the outlines
than he felt he could ever learn in passive reading,
and the completed outlines became a unique, personal source
for future reference.

3. *The Retreat System*

Friend "C" concentrated hard on scriptures
during his mission, only to
come home, quickly get married, quickly become a father,
progress rapidly in his business . . .
all of which stopped his scripture study.
He decided that intense bursts of serious study
were better than superficial "five-verses-a-day" programs,
so he and his wife started taking one weekend every two months

away from home and children and business and friends
to work on scriptures.
They studied by topic,
referencing and cross-referencing together,
and said that they learned more in two days
than they otherwise could in two months.

> (A by-product was a softer, clearer rapport
> between them
> after each trip.)

They called their system "vacation with a purpose."

4. *The Question-Exchange System*

Friends "D," another married couple, separated more than they
wished,
held a special private meeting
each Sunday
in which they reported to each other on
what they had learned from scriptures during the week,
and each asked a question (the hardest they could find)
to test the other's knowledge and
to promote discussion.

5. *Spiritual Food before Physical*

Friend "E" had tried all the systems,
and kept slipping, forgetting, neglecting, discontinuing,
so he opted for something simpler.
He just resolved never to eat until he'd read.
He committed each day to take on at least a taste of
spiritual scriptural food
before taking a bite
of physical breakfast food.
His appetite became the motivator
for a consistent scripture habit.

Learning through Prayer

We don't think enough of prayer
as a learning experience.
We thank God, and we ask him for things,
      but seldom, too seldom,
      do we ask for knowledge and *learn* through prayer.

One missionary companion of mine,
named John,
learned the gospel from the Spirit . . .
directly . . .
without books, without study.

He had been converted to the Church one winter
while away at college.
His bishop there called him on a mission,
to leave the next fall after a summer
of preparation and study at home in Wyoming.

But John's father resisted the Church
so strongly
that he threw the books out and
allowed no more in.
      John, with nothing to study,
      was to prepare himself by fall.

He worked all summer with his antagonistic father
on their farm,
      shoulder to shoulder
      but without a word.
John thought as he plowed,
prayed as he sowed,
contemplated as he milked the cows.

John didn't know the scripture in Doctrine and Covenants 88,
but he was following it.
He was "seeking learning by faith" . . .
exclusively by faith, because he had nothing else!

Answers came.
        As he crawled under a fence or
        hoisted a hay bale,
        he thought of his question of the day before
        and found that it was no longer a question . . . that
        the Spirit
        had answered it.

When he left in the fall, his father told him
that if he was going on a mission
he need not bother
to ever come home.

John went . . .
and became one of the greatest missionaries of my experience.
He studied the scriptures in the mission field . . .
not only to gain knowledge
but also to document and scripturally locate
truths that
he already knew.

When you ask for knowledge or insight,
the Lord will expect you to study and analyze first,
but he *will* guide you to an answer.

A prayer for truth should
be approached the way you would approach an interview
for advice with some great and reverend person.
You would never walk into the home of
the man you perceived as great without
substantial preparation.

And after asking your questions
you would never walk out without waiting
for his answer.
Too often we do both in our "interviews" with God.

By pushing the earthly comparison a little further,
we can see the importance and power of faith in our prayers.
If you were asking a great man
for help of some kind,
your faith in his ability to help you could
exist on three levels.
1. Faith that the man exists, lives, can be contacted by you.
2. Faith that he has the necessary knowledge, ability, and power to
help you.
3. Faith that he likes you enough and thinks you are deserving and
important enough to have his help.

Faith in God, of course, works on the same levels.

To go still a step further . . .
the process of asking a great man for
advice or help would probably include:

      1. *Reflection* and planning with regard to
      what your need is and *how* to
      make the request of him.

      2. *Analysis or thought* about the nature
      of your request—what is involved?
      Why do you need the help? What are your motives?

      3. *Appreciation* expressed to him for other
      help he has given you previously and for his
      taking the time to listen to this request.

      4. *Asking* as humbly and directly as possible for
      the thing you need.

5. *Commitment* that you will do your part
to live the laws that govern the success of
your request.

6. *Expressions of faith* and of belief
that the man can help you.

7. *Follow-through and action* on the advice you
receive.

Asking God should follow the same pattern . . . but with
a far greater feeling of love . . . for in prayer
we are approaching the *greatest* being . . .
and we are approaching our *Father.*

Learning by Inspiration

Inspiration is often the product of prayer
and can be the result of
personal questions asked of God.

Some knowledge can be gained only by direct inspiration,
because it is nowhere else available.
The right answers to important personal decisions . . .
The understanding and direction of our foreordinations . . .
The best way to fulfill our callings . . .
all are in the category of personal knowledge
that is relevant only to us
and may not be specifically recorded in scripture
or specifically available through advice from other people.

In these things we must go directly to the Lord.
In matters relating to our own stewardships
there is no middle link
between ourselves and God.

We need to make our Heavenly Father
our *chief* confidant.
We need to *ask* him in all things.
We need to share problems and secrets and concerns
with him more often
       and more fervently than with
       anyone else.

Too often we overlook the source
           of greatest strength,
           of greatest wisdom,
           of greatest solace,
and we suffer and carry our burden alone
even though he is willing and able to help.

He asks us to ask.

And his answers distill on our souls like dew.
Dew appears on the grass
from no apparent direction or source.
It is just there, glistening,
wet and perfect.
God's answers come similarly . . . suddenly or slowly,
but usually softly and subtly.
We ask,
we work and watch and wait,
and then, they are there.

Learning from Others

Contrast in your mind the numbing, dulling experience
of an evening watching television
with the exhilarating, awakening experience
of an evening spent with people you admire.

That makes me think of one other lesson learned from my
old tennis coach.
He said:
"If you want to improve, always play
with people who are better than you are."

The principle works as well in life.
>If you want to improve your mind,
>expose it as often as possible to *great* minds
>(either directly or through books).
>If you want to improve your leadership ability,
>expose yourself to great leaders.
>>In this sense we all need heroes.
>>We need ideals and people we wish to emulate.
>>The "ideal idol" is someone you hold in high
>>esteem . . .
>>but also someone accessible enough that you can have
>>personal contact and interaction with that person.

Some have the problem of having no idols,
but more have the problem of having no direct contact
or learning opportunity with those whom they do admire.
We should learn that great people usually are
flattered by being admired . . . by being asked for
advice or counsel.

Therefore, expose yourself to greatness.

Broaden your association base . . .
associate with people
you like and admire for different reasons.

The first year I spent at
a well-known Eastern school of business administration
was a little narrow and a little less than fulfilling
because I was surrounded
every day
by people with the same orientation,
              the same approach,
              the same norms,
              the same patterns of thought,
              the same objectives.

The second year at the same place,
I discovered other graduate schools,
made friends among architects and artists,
              historians and humanists,
              psychologists and philosophers,
              scientists and sociologists.
I found there was nothing more refreshing,
after a day of "critical path charts" and "economic models,"
than to talk with a painter
about "color values" and "form sketches."

Too much learning or too much orientation in one area
is dangerous as well as dulling.
Sophisticated management has found that the best
problem-solving group is not a homogeneous group of
like-thinking business professionals
but a heterogeneous group . . . a builder,
a chemist, a musician,
a merchant, a teacher . . .
Each sees the same problem from a different perspective
and thus the answers derived are
fuller, more comprehensive,
more usable in the real world.

This lifetime is a time so precious,
a time so limited,
that we must spend it well . . . and "prioritize" it to learn
the things we cannot learn later
(or the things that will be harder
to learn in some other realm of existence).

It is ironic that some people devote every waking
hour to the study of some earthly field of knowledge
(which can probably be more quickly and more accurately
learned in the spirit world)
and thus devote almost *no* time to the
things we were *sent to this earth to learn* . . .
such as:
1. How to live by faith and form a relationship with Christ
and with God the Father.
2. Family unity and happiness.
3. Nature and its beauty, and how to live in harmony with it.
4. How to understand and help and relate to other people.
5. The gospel and its application in life.
6. How to perfect ourselves and repent.
7. How to depend on God.
8. How to forgive and forget.
9. How to be good stewards over our bodies, our
children, our appetites, our challenges, our
opportunities, our material things, our knowledge,
our talents, our moods, our freedom.

Learning by Sagacity

Sagacity is a great word.
As mentioned, it is a prerequisite and prompter of serendipity.
It is sensitive, insightful *awareness.*
It is seeing with wisdom.

Watch a beaver building sometime
and see what you learn;
or watch clouds,
or bees,
or trees.

Learn by conscious observation of all things,
but most particularly
of nature.

There is no more interesting thing to study than nature . . .
and no more valuable thing to understand.
Christ tells us that all things (which he made) testify of him.
While you are observing,
remember
that *people* are a part of nature . . .
the most important part, really . . .
the part that the other parts were made for.
The closer you come to understanding people and their
motives and feelings, the closer *your* knowledge is to *God's*.
Be an astute observer of people.

You might not come in contact
with enough beavers or bees to really know them,
but no one can say that about people!

Another way of saying "understanding nature"
is to say "understand Joy 1 and Joy 2."
Joy 1 comes out of the essence of *nature* . . .
bodies, earth, agency;
and Joy 2 revolves around and is dependent on
relationships and achievements that are
human nature . . .
Seek to understand Joy 1 and Joy 2.
Strive to be aware of them, to grasp their meaning,
to see them through the eternal lens of the gospel,
thus to turn them into Joy 3.

Pursuit of Joy 3—Overview

Again, the spiral diagram works.

More knowledge and insight

More Joy 3

Knowledge increases Joy 3 and
Joy 3
motivates us to pursue more knowledge.

9

The Sealer of Joy

Righteousness and the Holy Ghost

1. The Vehicle of Joy
Our second estate—
earth, bodies, agency
(physical)

2. The Enhancers or Prompters
Relationships and
accomplishments
(social/emotional)

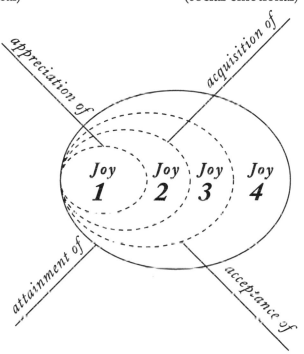

4. The Sealer of Joy
Righteousness and
the Holy Ghost
(Spiritual)

3. The Expander of Joy
Knowledge, truth,
and testimony
(mental/spiritual)

Six Stories: Part Four

Use your fingers again to hold your place
at page 21, page 58, and page 110,
so that you can review the earlier portions of each story.

"The Flower and the Camera"—Part Four

Now something of a botanist and a photographer,
you grasp and keep and share more
of what is around you.
One day, in scripture you read of lilies of the field
and feel the metaphorical and spiritual part
of the beauty
in a new, sealed part of your heart.

"The First Lawn Mowing"—Part 4

Each of the other joys seems insignificant
compared to what happens when Dad
comes home, looks at the lawn,
picks his sons up—one in each arm—holds them close and says,
"Boys, what a great job! I'm so proud of you."
Boys grow,
lawn becomes life,
and someday
Heavenly Father
says, "Well done."

"The Love Story"—Part Four

As they lived their life together,
John and Mary grew to love the Lord as well as to know him.
They repented of past errors together;
they worked hard and consciously at
        working out their own salvation.
They sought the Lord's will diligently and daily,
and combined their best efforts with his help in doing that will.

They learned to make themselves capable
of receiving and retaining the Holy Ghost's presence.
They refined themselves until they
could conduct the power and current of the Holy Ghost
with much less of the resistance that impurities always cause.
Over the years they became vessels of increasing purity,
and the Holy Ghost sealed and promised
the validity of all ordinances and covenants they had made
and assured them of their sanctification through Christ.

"The Marriage"—Part Four

As the marriage ceremony is performed
by the authority of God,
the Spirit of God intensifies in the room,
and moist eyes are the exterior reflection
of true internal joy.
Suddenly there is no question of the divine source of joy . . .
no concern that it is imagined or that it
will disappear when they walk out into daylight.
The Spirit whispers
the Lord's acceptance and pleasure with what is occurring,
and thus
joy changes by *kind* as well as by *degree*
and is no longer dependent
on the sunshine or
the pleasant circumstances of life.
The Holy Ghost has sealed the joy and lifted it
from the world's realm to a heavenly sphere.

"The New Arrival"—Part 4

The emotion and feelings move you to tears,
and there, in the privacy of the hospital room,
you close your eyes and thank the Lord
for it all.

Through the prayer's effect, the Holy Ghost
fills your heart
and whispers to your mind the assurance
that God is pleased with your life and with
your efforts to serve him.
Your joy now expands into spiritual realms.
The Holy Ghost's presence transcends earthly feeling
and seals and sanctifies your joy,
leaving you basking in the ultimate reality
of Joy 4.

"The Promotion"—Part Four

The next Sunday—planning, praying, realizing that
the real questions are why and what.
Why have I been this blessed and
what is expected of me—by God?
It's more than a price or an accomplishment.
It's a stewardship, an opportunity, an obligation.
I now have more to be grateful for:
> more chances to set an example that will be seen,
> more people to look out for,
> more opportunity to serve.

The thoughts bring the Spirit.
I feel his pleasure
in what I've done and in what I plan to do.

Joy 4 Is Complete Joy

As part four of each story illustrates,
it is the Holy Ghost
> that completes joy . . .
> that makes it full . . .
> that makes it lasting . . . and
> that makes it independent of the circumstances
> and fortunes
> of the world.

Only those who possess all four elements of joy
(their second estate, their relationships and achievements,
their knowledge and gospel insight,
and the companionship of the Holy Ghost)
can feel joy in all circumstances . . .
> clouds or sun,
> failure or success,
> poverty or wealth.

Joy 4 is independent of and above them all.
Imagine a modern-day Job (see Job 1:13–20),
a man who possesses
Joy 1 and Joy 2 in abundance . . .
A successful man with many possessions,
with a dear and close family,
with health and freedom . . . surrounded by beauty.

Then it is taken away.
He loses health, family, possessions,
his friends desert him,
his life crumbles around him through no fault of his,
and all seems lost.

Now let's give him the elements of Joy 3 . . .
of gospel truths and insights,
so that he knows his body will be renewed,
     his family will be reunited,
     his heavenly wealth will exceed
          all he knows . . .
so that he understands the place and the purpose of testing
              and of adversity.

Will it help? Surely, but not enough
to turn his heartaches to joy.
Only God can turn sorrow to joy (John 16:20).
Only God can give joy in times of affliction (1 Thessalonians 1:6).
Only the Comforter,
     the Spirit of truth, the Holy Ghost
          can calm him,
          can give him solace, and can
          make his comprehension *deep* enough
          to understand the possible reasons
          and to anticipate future glory.

Even Peter, whom Christ called the rock,
was weak and frail
     (to the point of denying thrice)
before he received the Holy Ghost.

The influence of the Holy Ghost
is as clearly recognizable
as a close friend
and as easy to distinguish from Satan's spirit
as a friend from an enemy.

The Holy Ghost's influence is
calm,
clear,
close,
warm,
enlightening,
clarifying,
comforting,
while Satan's spirit and influence is

                    nervous,
                    upsetting,
                    unrestful,
                    confusing,
                    dark,
                    cold,
                    agitating.

The influence of the Holy Ghost
has such profound impact on
the other three levels of joy that it changes them
not only in degree
but in kind.

Consider, for example, what the Lord's Spirit can do
to the body (and hence to Joy 1).
Parley P. Pratt wrote:

> "The Holy Ghost . . . quickens all the intellectual
> faculties, increases, enlarges, expands and purifies
> all the natural passions and affections; and adapts
> them, by the gift of wisdom, to their lawful use.
> It inspires, develops, cultivates and matures all
> the fine-toned sympathies, joys, tastes, kindred
> feelings and affections of our nature. . . . It develops
> beauty of person, form and features. It tends to health,

vigor, animation, and social feeling. It invigorates all the faculties of the physical and intellectual man."[1]

Consider as another example how the Lord's Spirit completes
Joy 2 by turning the two-way limited partnership
of marriage
into a three-way unlimited partnership.

Consider, as a final example, how the Lord's Spirit works on
Joy 3 by imparting knowledge that is unavailable from
any other source . . .
knowledge of foreordination and personal purpose . . .
insight into the workings and
feelings and objectives of God.

Quite often, when Paul spoke of or experienced joy,
he connected it to the presence of the Holy Ghost.
We read that . . . the fruit of the Spirit is love,
joy, peace (Galatians 5:22).

. . . the power of the Holy Ghost allows
us to abound in hope, peace,
joy (Romans 15:13).

. . . people in affliction received
the *joy* of the Holy Ghost
(1 Thessalonians 1:6).

Glimpses of the Joy of the Holy Ghost

There are some fleeting glimpses of Joy 4
in the different contexts
of the beautiful and varied ways that
God's Spirit works on ours.

---

1. *Key to Theology*, p. 101.

Picture a businessman who has had
          a trying and difficult week,
who crossed the country and back
for the unpleasant purpose
of closing an office and selling part of his company.
He gets back, tired and turmoiled,
on Saturday night.
In the morning he takes his family to church,
partakes of the sacrament, renews covenants,
finds a calmness, a peace, a joy—
     and this because the Holy Ghost
     is the Spirit of peace and the peacemaker.

Imagine next a college freshman,
new on campus and a little green,
anxious to do well . . .
facing her first major exam . . .
knowing that she has studied the material well,
not knowing if she can remember it accurately
          or write it coherently.
She retires in secret prayer,
     in a secret place,
and asks for help in an area where she has tried
       hard to help herself . . .
       in an area where she believes
       achievement is worthwhile.

The Holy Ghost strengthens her, clears her memory,
and gives joyful confidence to her mind—
       and this because the Holy Ghost
       is the Spirit of *confidence* and
       strength.

Envision now a person new in his career.
He looks at himself and at his world
and wonders how they fit together.
He goes for advice to people he respects,
and ultimately to God.

Through an earnest struggle of analysis and fasting and prayer
he comes to a decision
regarding which job to take . . .
and through a second prayerful struggle
the Holy Ghost causes his bosom to burn with joy,
confirms the correctness of his choice—
        and this because the Holy Ghost
        is the Spirit of guidance and of gifts and of the
        revelation of foreordination.

        The Holy Ghost will show you
        all things you should do (2 Nephi 32:5).

        The Holy Ghost will give you the
        gifts that apply to your
        foreordination—different
        gifts to different people (Moroni 10:8, 17).

Imagine next a funeral,
grieving friends and family
individually and collectively asking why.
The service progresses, the Spirit flows.
Grief intermingles with hope and love and light,
even with a kind of joy—
        and this because the Holy Ghost
        is the Comforter.

Think next of
a young couple
looking for direction . . . aware of
the magnitude of the responsibility
of their new little family . . . anxious for answers.

They meet two young men in dark suits
who say they have a message . . .
a church that is complete, practical,
true.

150

They look into it, visit it, listen to its teachings, read them,
and, finally,
live them and pray about them.

Testimony comes not with brass and cymbals,
but with quiet joy, with compelling, absolute sureness
from the Holy Ghost's spiritual whisperings—
  and this because the Holy Ghost
  is the Spirit of truth
  and bears the strongest testimony of all.

 Joseph Fielding Smith said:
 "The spirit of God speaking to the spirit of man
 has power to impart truth with greater effect and
 understanding than the truth can be imparted by
 personal contact even with heavenly beings.
 Through the Holy Ghost the truth is woven into
 the very fibre and sinews of the body
 so that it cannot be forgotten."[2]

Picture this time in your mind:
A noted scientist
fighting for a formula to fight a disease.
He experiments, analyzes, tests, examines,
but nothing in his own mind and
nothing produced by his logical or analytical abilities
gives him the answer.
He is earnest in his efforts; he seeks the answer
for the good of mankind.
One day
(in retrospect he believes his mind was wandering),
suddenly a snap—a connection he hadn't considered . . .
the joyous answer
in a flash of what he can only call inspiration—
  and this because the Holy Ghost
  is the revealer of truth.

---

2. *Doctrines of Salvation*, 3 vols., comp. Bruce R. McConkie (Bookcraft, 1954), 1: 47–48.

James E. Talmage wrote, speaking of the Holy Ghost:

"Not a truth has ever been
made the property of humankind
except through the power of that great Spirit."[3]

Imagine now a great artist of any kind . . .
a painter, a poet, a sculptor, a composer . . .
He feels something and
wants to say it through
his medium
to others.
If his feeling and his desire are deep enough
he may feel a transcending insight . . .
a lightning-quick, crystal-sure mental grasp of joy
that opens and frees his mind;
and he creates something that he knows *he*
didn't really create—
      and this because the Holy Ghost
      is light
      and can illuminate the mind
      to the level
      of pure creativity.

Think of a man and his wife
emerging from the hospital
with their firstborn babe . . .
impressed and humbled by the persistent, joyful feeling
that this child is also a sister . . .
one whose existence started not at mortal birth,
                but long before—
      and this because the Holy Ghost
      is the penetrator of the veil . . .
      the one who gives us glimpses
      of what went before.

3. *Articles of Faith* (Deseret Book, 1984), p. 149.

Finally, try to envision
a man and wife, angry and arguing,
each seeing only one view and protecting it . . .
getting further apart, more self-centered, more critical,
less tolerant, less tender
with each word.
Finally, in a brief burst of humility and desperation
driven to their knees . . .
praying, first haltingly, with difficulty . . . then, finally,
freely, fluently, openly . . .
"O, Lord, help us, for we seem unable to help ourselves . . .
let us understand each other."
The dark, nervous, contending, "out-taking" spirit of contention
leaves . . .
the light, sweet, forgiving, calm, "out-giving" spirit of the Holy
Ghost
comes . . .
and
suddenly, joyfully,
he sees her viewpoint, and she sees his,
so clearly that they almost shift sides
and sponsor the other's view.
Both now look for ways to comfort the other,
                                    to make the other happy—
        and this because the Holy Ghost
        is the conciliator . . .
        His presence makes anger and hate impossible,
        makes love and compassion automatic
        and deep
        and genuine.
There is great Joy 4 in each of these feelings
and in the *knowledge*
of our dependency upon it.

Four Levels of the Spirit

People feel the influence of the Holy Ghost
on all different levels, to all different degrees,
and the "he-draws-closer-as-you-draw-closer" notion
is accurate . . .
but there are four definable general levels
that can be used to categorize
our relationship to the Spirit of God.
Interestingly, they correspond rather closely
with the four levels of joy.

Level 1:

> The "light of Christ" burns at *some* level
> in all men—some call it conscience
> or morality or inherent humanism.
> Our actions determine its intensity
> but it does *exist* in all.
> It is this element of light . . .
> this pinhole opening to our origins and to
> the Spirit of Him who created us . . .
> that makes even the basest, coarsest person
> responsive to beauty and
> sometimes aware
> of Joy 1.

Level 2:

> The influence of the Holy Ghost
> can be available to all; indeed, the Spirit
> is willing to come to all in moments
> when their souls are hungry enough and their
> desires righteous enough to receive him.
>
> A mother who deeply feels the need for help
> in counseling her child
> and who prays for that help . . .

The seeker of truth who finds the gospel
and earnestly wants to know if it is true . . .
even if his prayer starts,
"O God, if there is a God."

One urgently needing comfort
or earnestly seeking truth
has access to the Comforter,
to the Spirit of truth,
but the Spirit's presence is fleeting
and hard to remember accurately once it is gone.

Level 3:
Those who extend their faith
to the point of righteous action
and of repentance
and who make the commitments and covenants
of baptism
can have the *gift* of the Holy Ghost.

Indeed the three-step process of faith,
repentance, and baptism
has as its purpose
the preparation of the individual
for the reception of the Holy Ghost.

Paul, aware of that purpose, retaught and rebaptized
some who had not received the Holy Ghost
following their first baptism (Acts 19:1–7).

When this great Spirit is *given*
as a *gift* from God
through the hands and words of one ordained with *his*
power, the recipient
has the *right* to the *constant* companionship of
the Holy Ghost so long as he or she lives righteously.

Oh, the joy that could be ours
if we exercised that option
and magnified that right!

Level 4:
> When it does happen ... when
> a person has the constant or at least consistent
> presence of the Holy Ghost ...
> that individual is drawing very close to
> the "Holy Spirit of promise," which is
> the witness of the Holy Ghost that
> an ordinance is valid and binding in heaven.
> All ordinances need this promise of confirmation
> before they are fully consummated.
>
> As we receive the Holy Spirit of promise,
> so may we develop and grow to the point where we are able
> to have our calling and election
> made sure and
> to have the ultimate Joy 4 available on this earth ...
> the joy
> of *knowing*
> that our lives are acceptable to God
> and that our eternal place with him
> is reserved.

The point is that
this pinnacle of joy is not something that
suddenly manifests itself and is instantly obtained ...
rather, it is the final rung in
a long ladder that gradually climbs
toward the more consistent and frequent
presence of the Holy Ghost.

You start with the light of Christ
and climb through various stages . . .
feeling God's pleasure with certain facets of your life,
then with more and other facets . . .
gaining a larger and clearer portion of the Holy Ghost's
influence as you go along . . .
striving toward the ultimate goal of exaltation
and the earthly assurance of it.
This is a long process,
but it is the way and the direction and
the only passage
to this earth's greatest fulfillment
        and most valuable reward . . .
                the presence and light of Joy 4.

10

The Pursuit of Joy 4

While all four levels of joy are *gifts*
from God to our spirits,
Joy 4 is the one that can
only be given spiritually and can
only be pursued spiritually.

We can go after Joy 1, Joy 2, and Joy 3
through our own physical and mental effort.
We can buff up our bodies through exercise
and get out and enjoy earth and nature.
We can set goals and plans and work hard
to achieve things and form relationships.
We can study and research
to understand God's word and life's purpose.

We can obtain and develop the stuff of Joy 1, Joy 2, and Joy 3
by *working* and *planning*.
But Joy 4 comes so exclusively as a gift
that we need different "W" and "P" words.
Instead of *work* and *plan*,
we must employ
watch and *pray*,
wait and *perceive*,
wonder and *ponder*,
worship and *praise*,
warmth and *peace*,
and remember that all is
wrought by *prayer*.

The ultimate power and assurance of God
comes gradually,
by degree:

    1. The light of Christ . . .
    2. The fleeting touches of the Holy Ghost . . .
    3. The gift of the Holy Ghost . . .
    4. The true receiving and "catching" of the Holy Ghost . . .
    5. The Holy Spirit of promise . . .
    6. The more sure word of prophecy . . .
    (calling and election made sure) . . .
    (the Second Comforter).

How to get on that staircase?
How to climb it?
How to reach number 6?

While it may
sound like an oversimplification . . . like a "too basic" way
to explain how to pursue the
greatest joy of all . . .
the simple rule is
to *want* the Holy Ghost's presence.

Those who *want* it badly enough
will get it,
because their wanting
will lead them to the two actions that bring it and instill it:

1. Asking for it.
2. Receiving it.

But before getting into each of those,
let's ask the question *why*.
Why don't people want it badly enough to
seek it?

Why don't people . . . particularly those who
have been given the gift
     of the right
          to his constant companionship . . .
               Why don't they seek it?
               Why don't they
               exercise that right?

Two answers:
     1. They don't know how to seek it.
     2. They are too busy seeking other things,
          things of the world . . . the approval of others.

In the final analysis,
     there's no excuse for either answer.
          The way to seek it is available
          in scripture and in the Church;
          and those who prioritize the seeking of other things
          will end up finding other things
          at the expense of their salvation.

Now let's look back to
the two actions
necessary to have the companionship of the Holy Ghost
(asking and receiving).

Asking for the Spirit

Imagine yourself as a father
who possesses a great gift . . . a gift
you would like to give your son . . .
but imagine also that there are certain laws
that prevent you from giving it to him
until he *asks* for it
     and until he meets certain conditions.

Thus you encourage him to ask . . .
you promise him that he will *receive* if he asks . . .
all this and yet,
for some reason (either pride or ignorance
or a simple lack of interest),
he won't ask.

You of course would continue to wish that
                      he *would* ask
and,
if he ever did
(and if he met the conditions necessary),
you would give him the gift as fully and as quickly as possible.

There is probably no gift that our Heavenly Father
would rather give us
than the Holy Ghost,
because he knows that the Holy Ghost is the ultimate help
in *his* objective
of bringing about our salvation and eternal life (Moses 1:39).

The Holy Ghost is a gift
that doesn't come all at once . . . and a
gift that doesn't stay forever once it comes.
      Thus we need to ask not once
      but *recurrently* . . . throughout our lives . . . and
            thus we need to be righteous not only once
            but progressively more so throughout our lives.

Too often we ask for the Spirit
only from the depths of our crises or our problems.
      When things go well, we feel self-confident
      and self-assured and unaware of our need
      for a greater strength.

Then when problems and crises come, we momentarily
realize our frailty,
our extreme need,
and then we ask.
       The answering Spirit
       lifts us,
       strengthens us,
       and we solve our problem . . . overcome our trial.

Then we are back to where we came in:
confident,
forgetful of our need for the Spirit,
and the cycle starts over again.

The result of this recurring cycle is that we drop as far as
we have climbed,
and our pattern looks like this:

Each peak is the same altitude as each previous peak.
There is no cumulative progress because
the feeling of the Holy Ghost
can't really be
remembered or recalled or recreated . . .

It is remembered
only when it comes again.

If you constantly maintain your awareness
of your dependence on God
and *ask* for the Holy Ghost
(even when things are going well),
you can break out above this cycle.
You will certainly slip at times, but your pattern will be:

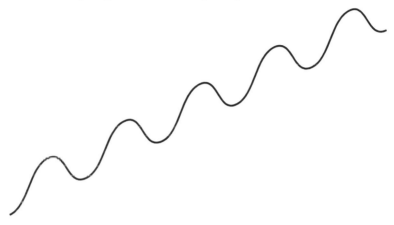

The strength you receive
through God . . . through asking . . .
can then be used to help others and
to build God's kingdom
rather than being dissipated in your own crisis.

After you have asked God,
ask yourself some questions:
      Where is the Holy Ghost usually felt?
      Why is he felt?
      What actions usually bring about his presence?

One who can answer those questions
has the knowledge necessary to increase Joy 4.
      If the Spirit is usually felt in the temple
      and you want the Spirit more often,
      go to the temple more often.

If the Spirit is usually felt when you are serving others
and you want it more,
serve more.
If the Spirit is felt when you are righteous . . .
and so on.

As we sat with him once in a fireside meeting,
a great Church leader was asked what seemed to be
a very difficult and involved question:
    "How can I increase the Spirit's presence in my home?"
He gave us a straightforward one-liner that
none of us had expected and he left us to figure out
what he meant.
    He said:
    "Use the priesthood more often."

Too many of us ask to know the future . . .
ask to know our foreordination completely and
        to know our specific lifetime purpose.
        How much better it is to ask for the Holy Ghost's guidance
        in *getting* to those destinations.

I once had a friend whom I envied because of
the sureness of his lifetime goals.
He felt that he had had his foreordination revealed
to him . . . that he knew his exact lifetime calling
and merely had to plan
each step of his life to get there.
I envied . . . because I had never had that revelation
and could only get short-term nudges
                (which graduate school to go to . . .
                then later which job to take). I was often
sure of God's will for my next immediate step,
but never able to see how it fit into any longer-range
foreordination.

Then one day I was
at the Grand Canyon and heard a man
asking a ranger if there was guide service to
the bottom of the canyon.
The ranger said yes, leaving in three hours.
"But you can see Phantom Ranch from here," he said,
pointing far and deep to the bottom of the trail.
"You can go on your own if you wish."
          The man's reply gave me an insight.
          He said, "Thanks, but I'd rather have a guide
          who would show the way
                    along the way
          than to just be told the destination."

Receiving the Spirit

Since we all differ, and each of us has
separate shortcomings,
it requires *asking* to know the specific
and individual conditions
we must meet to merit the Spirit.

However,
the *general* conditions and prerequisites are known.
The conditions are the commandments.
The prerequisites are the principles
of the gospel.
When we obey the commandments
          and live the principles,
we acquire a key called righteousness . . .
          a key that opens the way to the
          presence and influence of the Holy Ghost.

The scriptures make clear the connection
between righteousness and joy.

. . . Joy in heaven when one sinner repents (Luke 15:7)
. . . A wise steward shall have joy (D&C 51:19)
. . . Meekness increases joy (Isaiah 29:19)
. . . Receiving Christ without seeing him brings joy
        unspeakable (1 Peter 1:8)
. . . The joy of giving up all one has for the gospel (Matthew 13:44)
. . . Joy comes to those who are forgiven for their sins (Mosiah 4:3)

Paul, speaking to the Romans,
put it all together (the joy of righteousness and of the
Holy Ghost)
in one line.
He said that the kingdom of God is
"righteousness, and peace, and joy in the Holy Ghost"
(Romans 14:17).

The path of righteousness
leading to the destination of the Holy Ghost
is well marked, well defined,
and has three major landmarks:
        Faith
        Repentance
        Baptism

When we add these to the gift of the Holy Ghost we have
the most basic statement of the gospel.
        We call it
        the first four principles.

Faith is a belief strong enough
to bring about action.
(It's also the *power* of working by mental/spiritual effort.)

The *types* of action faith brings about are:

1. Obedience
    (not blind obedience to arbitrary laws,
    but faithful obedience to the loving
    counsel given to us by a wise Father)
2. Sacrifice
    (giving up ourselves and things of ourselves
    in favor of others and God
    and the things of God)

3. Gospel knowledge and compliance
    (understanding the positive "thou shalt"
    concepts of the gospel and thinking in their
    realm rather than in the lower
    sphere of "thou shalt not")

4. Consecration
    (thinking of ourselves as stewards
    over things that belong to God . . .
    any of which we would willingly
    give up if he asked)

The exercise of faith should be an
enjoyable process.

Many associate somber dead seriousness with righteousness
                                and with faith.

That is strange, because a too-serious attitude
and the lack of a sense of humor
                tend to destroy *any* relationship,
                and faith *is* a relationship . . . with God.

When Joseph Smith was asked why he, a prophet,
laughed and joked and wrestled and did other
"unholy" things . . .
      He said that a bow had to be unstrung once in a while
              or it would lose its spring.[1]

G. K. Chesterton said that a characteristic of great saints
is their power of levity,
and he suggested
that angels can fly because they
have learned how to take themselves lightly.

Repentance must be a recurring process,
for it is with recurrence that we sin and err.
      When the wise old sage told the humble woman
      that repentance was like going to the garden
      and bringing the largest rock . . .
      then returning it to its exact original spot . . .
      he also told her self-righteous companion
      that repentance was like gathering a large bag
      of small stones
      and then returning each one to its precise original position.

To truly repent
we must think of the small things . . .
we must think in terms of overcoming
our sins of omission
as well as those of commission . . .
We must take seriously the
scriptural admonition
to be perfect
by perfecting ourselves one small step at a time . . .
We must help others and accept responsibility,
and remember that a pillar
is much harder to push over if it has
a building of responsibility resting on it
than if it is standing alone.

---

1. See *Juvenile Instructor*, 27:472.

The Spirit's power has often been compared
to electrical current
(although James E. Talmage said that was like comparing
a locomotive to a packhorse or an ocean liner to a raft of logs).[2]
Still . . . the comparison illuminates.
> The Spirit passes through the *contact* of one conductor
> to another . . . it flows like current, as it did
> when the woman in the crowd touched Christ
> and he felt virtue go out from him (Mark 5:30).

When a conductor is filled with impurities,
the current flow is resisted and
the resulting heat may destroy or break
the connection.
Similarly, when our lives are filled with
impurities
it is hard to have the Spirit and
impossible for the Spirit
to work effectively within us.

When a person with many impurities accepts the gospel, and
tries hard to accept the Spirit,
it is likely that the spiritual current will be strong
enough to burn out the impurities
(by causing repentance).
This "burning out" process may explain
the fire and emotional spirituality of those
who have just received the gospel.
> Later, when the conductor is burned pure, it
> can conduct even greater amounts of current (spirit)
> with complete calmness and little resistance.

We can and must burn out our impurities . . . and we must
remember our need to be working out our own salvation
before we can help others work out theirs.

---

2. *Articles of Faith*, p. 161.

Following repentance comes *baptism,*
which,
in its physical act, is a symbol
>   (but a symbol important enough that Christ himself
>   insisted on experiencing it),
and which, in its spiritual reality, is the
literal removal of our sins.

Through the sacrament of the Lord's Supper
each week
we can renew our baptism
by renewing the three covenants of baptism:
>   1. taking upon us His name,
>   2. remembering His life and teachings,
>   3. keeping His commandments.
Each of the three sounds simple enough . . .
but in fact each is deep and profound
and holds meaning on several levels.
Take the second one:
>   How do we remember
>   the Savior's life and teachings
>   if we don't *know*
>   his life and teachings?
>   And how can we know
>   his life and teachings
>   if we don't study them
>   extensively and
>   carefully?

The Holy Ghost,
the sealer and sanctifier of joy,
comes to those who seek . . .
to those who ask . . .
to those who receive.

There is nothing more critical to pursue
or
more rewarding to find.

Postscript

Try It!

The message of this book
        is that joy can be pursued and discovered
                sequentially . . . one level at a time.

In reflection, I find that I am most familiar with Joys 1 and 2
and I testify to their magnificence.
A generous amount of Joy 3 has come into my life . . .
partially through my own effort,
but mostly through the gift and generosity of God.
I have glimpsed Joy 4 . . . now and again.
In circumstances that attract it I have felt its drops fall on me,
but I have not bathed in it, as I know some have.

If you think about it, you may find that
your experience is similar to mine.

Evaluate and determine where you are . . .
what level you are already at . . . and go from there.

You may find that you can reach Joy 1 quite quickly . . .
by a little polishing, a little heightened appreciation . . .
by awareness of some of the things in chapters 3 and 4.

Joy 2 may take a little more work, and Joy 3 may take a
lifetime,
and chapters 5 through 8 may help both you and me
                        along the way.

Joy 4 is the ultimate goal,
and somehow, something in chapters 9 or 10 may
                jog each of us a little closer to it.

Sample and become more personally aware
of the levels of joy
by focusing strongly and clearly on each
for a period.

Spend a month focusing on Joy 1.
> Be more aware and appreciative
> of body, of earth, of agency.

> Consciously use and maintain
> that body, that earth, that agency.

> Constructively discipline your appetites,
> your body, your earth, your agency.

You'll know Joy 1 when you get it
because
your body will seem more alive . . .
your agency will mean more to you than it ever has . . .
and your world will change from mono black and white
> to stereo, technicolor cinerama.

Then spend two months on Joy 2
> (don't misunderstand . . . it takes a lifetime . . .
> but two months of conscious emphasis can
> open its vision enough
> to prove that it is worth your effort).

> Set achievement objectives
> > (and sub-objectives)
> and plan and work and pray to achieve them.

> Write three-year-out relationship descriptions.
> Program yourself to relationship objectives.
> Plan and work and pray to achieve them.

Cultivate the attitudes of
"waves" and "lightning"
and learn how to nudge yourself into them.

Couple the prompters with the vehicle
and openly experience Joy 2.

Then spend three months on Joy 3 . . .
    three months in which you design and set
                a pattern
                that lasts through your life . . .
                a pattern of
                scriptural study learning,
                sagacious observation learning,
                sensitive "from-others" learning,
                sincere-question prayer learning,
                specific inspiration learning.

        Let the insight and understanding
        magnify Joy 2 into Joy 3.

Then spend four months on Joy 4
                by diligently asking for
                the Holy Ghost . . .
                and
                by working harder than you ever have on
                the qualifications
                of righteousness . . .
                by consciously starting the eternal process
                of becoming perfect
                on one commandment at a time.
After these ten months you will discover at least a
glimpse of the glory
of Joy 4 . . .
and you will know what its components are
and how to pursue each of them.

Try it.

Don't despair when it takes time.

Remember that joy is discovered during the pursuit
rather than at the end.

Remember that what you are pursuing is
the goal of this life.

Remember that pursuit
        will bring joy not only to you
        but to those around you . . .
        for joy
        (like certain other heavenly assets,
        and unlike any earthly assets)
        increases and multiplies
                    as it is given away.

About the Author

Richard Eyre, a former mission president in London, is the author or co-author of more than twenty-five books, including a *New York Times* #1 bestseller. He and his wife, Linda, have eleven children and live in Salt Lake City and Washington, D.C. He welcomes feedback at rickrick@arosnet.com.

**How knowing
where you came
from can change
who you are and
where you're
going…**

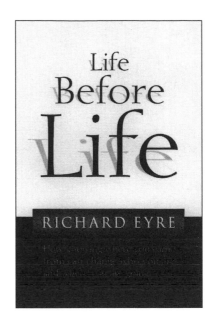

Our understanding of premortal life may be the most unique and powerful doctrine of the Restoration. Knowing you lived before can have a profound effect on your personal identity and on the sense of purpose you feel in life. In this groundbreaking new book, Richard Eyre explores the deeper implications of revealed answers to the ageless question, "Where did I come from?"

Life Before Life is a powerful yet intimate doctrinal exploration for Church members and an ideal gift to present to spiritually inclined nonmembers.